Did You See That? On The Outer Banks

Joe Sledge

Books by Joe Sledge
Did You See That? A GPS Guide To North Carolina's Out Of
The Ordinary Attractions
Did You See That? On The Outer Banks
Did You See That? Too!
Did You See That Ghost?
Haunting The Outer Banks
Bess Truly And Her Zap-Gun Rangers
Nag's Head: Or, Two Months Among "The Breakers"
By Gregory Seaworthy
Joe Sledge – editor

Did You See That? On The Outer Banks

A GPS Guide to the Out of the Ordinary Attractions
on the North Carolina Coast

Joe Sledge

Did You See That? On The Outer Banks

ISBN 978-0-9980968-4-1

Cover design by Barbara Noel.

To my parents, who brought their children to the sea.

Table of Contents

Introduction to the Second Edition

"When I was young growing up on the Outer Banks, every day was a vacation."

That's how I began the introduction to this book only a few years ago. It's funny how times change so fast. Has the Outer Banks changed that much in such a short time? Who would notice if it did? It certainly has seen a lot of changes and additions recently. There are new beaches, new bridges, new houses, and new people all coming to the islands. There is an ever incoming tide of visitors and residents, all ready to build their castle in the sand.

With all that is new comes the passing of the old. In the first edition of this book, I reminisced about my old beach house and my easygoing life as a kid on the shore. I find some of it still fitting. "Yes, life was easy, life was simple. Our biggest worry [as children] was closing the windows in time when the storms rolled in at night. Now, satisfaction is a little harder to come by. And we're not kids anymore. The big houses that litter the beach may have big TVs and big game rooms, and there are plenty of mini golf courses, complete with long waiting lines for people to visit all summer. But then there are some who want something a little different, or a lot different. There's still some weird old, and some weird new, stuff out there on the Outer Banks. This book will help you find it."

Yes, those days are long gone. Many parts of the beach are not as wildly adventurous as they were long ago. Luckily, there are still places to discover and explore along the Outer Banks. A rotten sunburn, a rainy day, or just a break from the family, all those are good excuses to go on an adventure.

Readers can still find some hidden bits of history in Did You See That? On the Outer Banks. There are lots of fun little side trips or scavenger hunts for kids and kids at heart. Some of these are true Did You See That? moments, where you elbow your friend in the ribs as you look on in surprise. They range from near the Virginia border, all the way up in Currituck's beaches, down through Kitty Hawk, Kill Devil Hills, and Nags Head, into Manteo, down to Hatteras and all the way past Ocracoke.

Whatever you use the book for, let it be a good reason to do some exploring and learning something new. Find something you never noticed before.

Going, Going... Gone!
A Note On The Updates

Sadly, we said goodbye to some of our Outer Banks. Progress is a double edged sword. Tides wash away the sandcastles. In this edition, I update a few of the subjects to mention that they are no longer there. I didn't want to just take them out entirely. For so many, it's fun to look back and remember what used to be. I wanted to preserve all the places I could, even if just in the pages of this book.

Several of the beautiful old Flat Tops, the original beach houses of Southern Shores, have been destroyed. The cozy single family retreats on large plots of land have been replaced by multi-family destination resort homes. Included in the loss of these wonderful little homes, once so distinctive of the Outer Banks, was Dunne's Dune. This home was a classic time capsule of a flat top house, and the one photographed in this book. So if you go looking for them using the GPS coordinates provided in this book, and find only a giant multistory house instead, know that the flat top met its end at the blade of a bulldozer.

No more will we see the funny face of Kilroy painted on the beach road in Kitty Hawk. The road suffers from flooding often, and was paved over. It is now a smooth black surface, a clean blank canvas. He may not have been much, but many of us knew he was there as we drove down the road, his eyes and nose peering over the line in the road like a fence, watching us as we went to the beach. "Wot, no sunscreen?"

The big Mako shark at Jennette's Pier came off the wall in a gust of wind. The damaged fish was removed and a replacement was put up. Other weather damaged items that have gone into protection include the original statues in the sunken gardens of the Elizabethan Gardens. The old statues of Roman gods were becoming too weather worn by the Outer Banks climate, and needed to be replaced. So, while something old might be gone, we still get something in their place.

Hopefully, these will be the last subjects that need to be updated in this book. Maybe soon, there will be a whole new book of strange places to visit. Until then... Good Hunting!

Oddity

A one to five star rating of just how strange the attraction is. Is it something you can see somewhere else? Or nowhere else? Does it fit in or stick out like a sore thumb? Just how odd, how unbelievable, does this place get? Well, this will help tell you.

*Please note that this rating guide is common to all Did You See That books, and not all books will have a chapter that meets every different rating.

★ It makes sense that this is here. I just didn't know about it. These are fitting for the locale, but may be hidden or unknown parts of history.

★★ You don't see that every day, unless you live here. Something different, but it still seems like part of the community. It may be less odd than one would think.

★★★ Whoa, how did they do that? It doesn't fit in, or it has a unique history about it. But, when you learn more about it, it's a little less weird I hope it doesn't come to life! These are the truly strange stories, places and legends that are hard to believe. It only gets stranger when you discover that the weird stories told about them are all true.

★★★★ I hope it doesn't come to life! These are the truly strange stories, places, and legends that are hard to believe. It only gets stranger when you discover that the weird stories told about them are all true.

★★★★★ I've never seen that before! Now, let's get outta here! These make the visitor truly uncomfortable. Scary, odd, or incredibly different, this doesn't belong, and you are probably not the only one who feels this way.

Difficulty

How hard is it to find the subject or get to it? Can you touch it? Do you even want to? This rating system will tell you how easy it is to find each location. Difficulty does not include distance from one town to another, or travel by ferry.

★ You can see it from the road. You don't really need to leave the car, if you don't want to. This also includes locations that have easily accessible parking lots.

★★ A little out of the way. This is going to mean a trip down a side road, or a little walking, but you can make it, right? This may include places that are only accessible at certain times.

★★★ Park and walk a ways. There may not be a path. There may be bugs. There could be some time issues with a location being available at the right time, such as being open only a few hours a week, or seasonally.

★★★★ Expect to be tired, a little sweaty. Or cold, depending on when you go. These spots may only be accessible for a short period of time. Some people may not want you there. You may need permission to visit or at least a reservation. This is going to be a hike.

★★★★★ You'll need tools, gear, specialized equipment, or the help of others just to get there. You may need permission, and it may not be coming. Going could get you in serious trouble, and you probably should just avoid this unless you are allowed, and you are extremely careful.

GPS Locations

The GPS coordinates supplied are approximate, but I have tried to make them as accurate as possible. The coordinates are based on Google Earth aerial maps, as well as handheld GPS units. I suggest you use Google Earth or other mapping tools to look up these locations, make sure the coordinates are accurate, and familiarize yourself with the nearby roads and parking areas before going. Also, make sure that these things are still there before you go looking, as sometimes they get relocated, taken away, or destroyed. Some may be in dangerous areas or on private property. Do not go into any area that would be dangerous for you. This book recommends that you always get permission to enter private property before visiting, or keep out.

The locations given are either on the actual spot, or on a nearby parking area, if available. Please note that driving on the Outer Banks can be difficult, as the roads easily get crowded, busy, and slow. I very highly recommend, urge, caution, whatever buzzword will sink in, that you keep your eyes on the road as well as the people and vehicles around you, rather than look for these places. Let someone else do the looking. And if you miss it, just keep going and turn around. Never slam on brakes to make a turn, never tailgate or drive too fast or awkwardly. Be conscientious, and courteous. Please realize that one important item about using a car based GPS is that it is made to give directions based on roads. It may try to bring you to a location that is not optimal for parking and walking to a spot in the woods or off a road. Consulting a map beforehand will allow you to be familiar with the location. If you need to, drive around until you find a good place to park and get out. This is why sometimes the coordinates are set for a parking area as opposed to the actual object. Once again, I suggest you use Google Earth as a guide before going.

Most auto GPS devices in North America will automatically put in the negative sign or the West notation for longitude. Online maps will not. When using coordinates on any computer map, use either N and W, or place a negative sign (-) by the longitude. If you do not do this, you end up in Tibet. No, really, you will. Or maybe Kashmir?

Penny's Hill/Lewark's Hill

Corolla 36.42825° -75.84015°

Long before paved roads became the norm along the Outer Banks, people needed the utilitarian four wheel drive truck to get from place to place, especially if work involved rutted passages through the scrub brush and sand that make up the barrier islands. But these off road vehicles also allowed access to places normally unvisited, like the beautiful beaches north of Corolla, and especially Penny's Hill.

Penny's Hill is a slowly meandering dune that imposes itself onto the northern part of Corolla. The dune and its blown out bowl have long been a popular place for 4-wheel drive vehicles to visit, both to drive up the dune, as well as to park and spend the day in its hard packed bowl, letting kids run and play. It even was the spot of an occasional field trip for young students to come after seeing the Currituck lighthouse, way before tourists could ever get that far.

But hidden under the dune, and also hidden in history, is another story. Hidden somewhere under Penny's Hill is an old town. And an old name.

Penny's Hill used to be part of Lewark's Hill, which sat near the fishing village of Seagull. Seagull was a prosperous little fishing village on the sound side of Currituck's Outer Banks. The town benefited from having deep creeks and a proximity to a major inlet from the ocean to the sound. Larger hulled boats could easily carry supplies around what is now Corolla, and ships could sail from inland ports through the inlet directly into the Atlantic Ocean. Just like the way port towns would go up around the mouth of a river, so Seagull grew with its water access. The little town had its requisite church, a school, and upwards of 30 houses at one time.

Seagull also benefited from popular outdoor activities of the day, namely hunting and fishing. Having the creeks and sound right at the back door, or probably front door, of the residents made it easy to take a boat out fishing. At the time, the Atlantic Flyway was the major thoroughfare for ducks and geese of all sorts, which brought hunters down from up north, looking for guides to help get to blinds and to recover the waterfowl they had taken. When federal regulations on hunting and fishing took hold in the 1920s, most residents left for the security of jobs in Virginia, especially into the Coast Guard, and the town began to slowly dwindle. After World War II, almost all families had moved, and the dunes began to take over the remnants of the town. Ultimately, the sand dune engulfed and covered what was left of Seagull, leaving no visible trace of the village.

Lewark's Hill and Penny's Hill were split in two sometime in the 1950s, when sand began to cover the town. And Penny's Hill took a big hit from the Ash Wednesday storm, which created the cut look to the dune, and washed much of the sand into the remnants of the Currituck Inlet. Penny's Hill lay to the north and what was left of Lewark's Hill was more to the south.

Now the sand from these dunes has moved so much that the remains of the town are starting to be uncovered on the other side of the hill. A part of the graveyard and a bit of chimney are peeking through the sand. But this is still hard to find. Lewark's Hill is pretty much gone now. The old town of Seagull would have sat south of current Penny's Hill. Any searching for the remnants of the old town should focus in this location. The area is still wild, with native animals and lots of thorny plant life to reach out to get you as you look. Even in spring and fall, it may be likely to run into snakes and biting varmints, raccoons or foxes, during explorations. Cooler days are better to look, with some of the scrub brush dying off, and fewer insects out and about, not to mention the lack of that Outer Banks summer sun beating down on you.

Oddity ★★★★

One of the houses in Seagull was owned by the family that gave their name to Lewark's Hill. John Lewark actually put his house on rollers in order to keep it out of the relentless march of the hill that bore his surname. Even moving it twice didn't stop the sand dune from consuming everything.

Difficulty ★★★★★

Ghost towns are hard enough to find when they aren't covered in sand. With storms and time often taking their toll on older houses along the coast, not to mention the relentless replacement of older houses with new, it's amazing there's anything to find. It took a giant sand dune to preserve what's left of this town. And, again, there are wild animals out there. It is highly likely to encounter a poisonous snake or a wild (and maybe rabid) animal out there. You'll either need a 4-wheel drive, or better yet, take one of the off-road tours offered in Corolla. You'll see a lot more, and you can let someone else do all the driving.

Monkey Island

Corolla 36.40479° -75.87011°

In the shallow waters of the Currituck Sound, mixed in with several other curiously named islands, sits a bit of tree and brush covered land called Monkey Island. The name goes back ages, to the Pomunkey natives that used the island as a hunting site. The Pomunkey tribe, which still exists in Virginia, was a hunter/gatherer tribe that would farm and hunt on land, then leave to other areas to let the land go fallow, and come back to it later. There still are the remnants of a Pomunkey burial ground on the northern tip of the island.

Monkey Island became a destination for hunters of a different sort sometime in the late 1800s, when the property was sold and became a hunt club for wealthy businessmen looking to come down from the North to shoot their fill of waterfowl. It attracted famous people of the day, not for its splendor, as this was less opulent than the more famous Whalehead Club, but for its isolation, which promised extremely good hunting.

The island and hunt club were owned by Charles Penn and his family from 1930, when he bought out other investors, up until 1974, when the island was sold to a venture corporation. Due to an economic recession, the Penn family was forced to buy it back, and finally sold the island to the Nature Conservancy, which then donated the land to U.S. Fish and Wildlife. During their ownership, Currituck County had a chance to restore the hunt club and use the island as an educational site, but the ongoing repairs needed and the concerns for safety made them change their minds.

And with good reason, it now seems. There is still a bit of the old hunt club on the island, with a fireplace intact in the main building, and the remnants of a dock and bulkheads as well, but it doesn't look all that inviting. Except to the birds, which have flocked back to the area now that the shotguns have gone silent. But the island does have some other, less desirable, occupants. Monkey Island never had monkeys on it, but today it is crawling with cottonmouth water moccasins, making a summer visit highly questionable. Today, the island is slowly returning to a more natural state, and is being partially reclaimed by the sound. The bulkhead that protected the land has long been decaying, and there is little left but some posts and slats sticking out of the water. NC Fish and Wildlife now use the island as a natural rookery for birds, and the land is protected. The island and its buildings can be seen from the water by boat. Wintertime, when the leaves are scarcer, might afford better viewing and slower snakes around the island.

Oddity ★

Any abandoned old building makes us a little curious about what's inside. The story that the rich and powerful would want to come down in the dead of winter makes it a little more strange.

Difficulty ★★★★★

Just don't go on the island. Just don't. It's not safe, there are snakes, there are old falling down buildings, there are birds that don't want to be disturbed. Lots of No Trespassing signs, too. A boat ride out to see it, from the water, is good enough.

Around the turn of the century, the Outer Banks had its vacation season reversed from what it is today. People would come down from up north in the winter for hunting., but no one wanted to stay there in the summer heat.

There actually is another Monkey Island, this one with real monkeys. Morgan Island, in South Carolina, is an isolated island that is used as a colony for free range rhesus monkeys used in laboratory experiments. The island was founded after monkeys escaped from an area in Puerto Rico, where they had been infected with the Herpes B virus. Eeeep! I'll take the cottonmouths!

Currituck Beach Lighthouse

Corolla 36.37664° -75.83066°

In 1872, noting the high number of ships lost along the coast near the North Carolina/Virginia border, the U.S. Lighthouse Board directed that a lighthouse be built on the area between Bodie Island and Virginia's Cape Henry Light. The light was especially beneficial to the southbound ships which had to hug the coastline in order to avoid the northbound freight train of water that was the Gulf Stream. In1873, construction on the lighthouse began, and was completed two years later.

From its beginning until 1939 the lighthouse was manned by keepers and their families from the keeper's quarters. Their jobs included pumping the oil for the lamp up to the 158 foot high lens, trimming the wick, and keeping the lens clean, among other chores and maintenance. In 1939, the lighthouse was automated, with the light turning on automatically at dusk to blink on for 3 seconds out of every 20.

By the 1970s, the keeper's quarters had been neglected and were in disrepair. The windows had broken, leaving the house open to the elements, and vandals. Outer Banks Conservationists began the process of restoring the building and grounds in 1980, and in October of 2003, the deed to the lighthouse was granted to OBC. People have been able to climb the lighthouse since 1991.

So, today people can make the drive up to Corolla to see the tall brick lighthouse, just like visitors and curious locals have been doing for years. Everyone knows all about this, right? What could entice someone to go up to the light, to find something new? Well, it could just be that the keeper's house is haunted.

Before the lighthouse was automated, keepers lived next to the light. The keeper's house was actually a duplex of sorts, two houses that shared a common center wall. They were usually mirror images of each other, but in this house, the north side has something that the south side doesn't have. The north room of the quarters is haunted. And wherever there is a haunting, there usually is a sad tale to go with it. But this place has more than one.

One of the first families of keepers at the light were George and Lucy Johnson, who had a daughter, Sadie. Being relatively isolated, Sadie would

spend her days at the beach building sandcastles on the shore. She would often come back soaking wet as she would play with her back to the ocean, where a breaking wave would sneak up behind her and splash her dress as she played. Sadly for the family, one day she didn't come back. Her body wasn't found until the next day, when it washed ashore and was discovered by a fisherman. It was in her bedroom, the north room, that she was laid for preparation of burial.

But that was only the first of a series of strange and depressing occurrences that happened in the north room. Once, a guest, a friend of the keeper's wife, who was staying in the north room, got sick and died under very mysterious circumstances. And an unknown keeper's wife was quarantined in the north room when she came down with tuberculosis. Tuberculosis was a dreaded disease, seen to be highly contagious, incurable, and deadly. It was no wonder she was isolated from the family. Soon, not being able to interact with the others in the house, she gave up the will to live and passed away. Fearing the disease, all of her personal items were sealed in a barrel and left in the room, because no one had any desire to touch them. The barrel even stayed once the quarters were abandoned and the light automated. Locals even told of a horrifying story of warning their children not to touch the barrel, that it was diseased, and they shouldn't play with it. This only led the local kids to do just that. They cracked open the barrel and played a macabre dress up with the dead woman's clothes, until terrified parents found out, gathered the garments and burnt them.

Since then, people have continually felt a presence in the north room. Some visitors who have been fortunate to tour the larger quarters have not been willing to set foot in the room. And even during renovation, some of the workers who did not even know of the legend were not willing to go into the north room, its gloomy otherworldly chill being so pervasive.

Haunted or cursed, there certainly is something weird with the north room of the keeper's quarters. So if someone asks you to stay overnight, and the north room is all that is left, politely decline. Just to be on the safe side.

Oddity ★

The lighthouse is not painted like other lighthouses are, and the brick color itself is used as a recognizable symbol for navigation. It also allows visitors to see just how many bricks went into the making of the lighthouse. Well, almost all. Of the approximately one million bricks, many are hidden within the walls. The base of the lighthouse is 5'8" thick.

Difficulty ★

Driving to Corolla is a long trip, with lots of other people heading that way, lots of people turning off and getting on the tiny road, but at least you can drive right up to the light. There is a fee for climbing the lighthouse. The lighthouse is open from late March until Thanksgiving, and may be closed during storms. If you want to climb the light, you may want to stretch first. It's a 158 foot climb to the lens, with 214 steps.

When it was first built, the lighthouse wasn't in Corolla. It was built in the village of Jones Hill. No, the lighthouse wasn't moved. When the town got big enough for a post office, the name was changed.

During the Cold War, certain buildings were studied to determine if they would be suitable for fallout shelters to protect people in the case of a nuclear attack and the radioactivity that would inevitably occur. The only places were considered adequate in Currituck County. One was an old vault at the county courthouse. The other was Currituck Light.

Whalehead Hunt Club

Corolla 36.37331° -75.83230°

The Atlantic Flyway is a veritable superhighway for migratory birds along the east coast of the United States. North Carolina's waterways and sounds are a popular stopover for waterfowl, with an abundance of shelter and food. Due to this, and a lack of obstructions on the path, the coast of the Outer Banks has a very high number of bird species passing through every year.

This, along with the relatively mild winter compared to up north, made the isolated lands in Corolla a popular place for northern businessmen.

Wealthy from the unchecked growth of the 1920s, they would come down to the peaceful seclusion of the NC coast. Among those industrialists was Edward Collings Knight, Jr., a railroad tycoon and hunter. He, along with his wife Marie Louise LeBel, would vacation on the coast over the fall and winter to hunt, enjoy the natural beauty, and escape the rampant development as well as cold that wrapped the northeast during the wintertime. The couple liked visiting so much they decided to build a private residence where they could spend the winters with a few friends while hunting and spending time in nature. They purchased a hunt club called the Lighthouse Club, renamed it Corolla Island, and set out to build a fancy and extremely exclusive hunt club on Corolla's sound side.

While most hunt clubs would be simple buildings, with a place to sleep and a fireplace to keep warm, Corolla Island had five fireplaces to heat the main rooms. In addition, the building also had a generator for electricity, oil heat for the rest of the house, an elevator, the first on the islands, and a swimming pool. A water pump was located in the boathouse to provide running water to all the guest rooms. Not truly a club, the building only had four guest rooms for close friends of the Knights. Once the necessities were out of the way, the Knights went on to decorating and furnishing the house with Tiffany lamps, and various Art Nouveau designs throughout the club.

The kitchen is unique in that it was done entirely in pink. Pink tile to go with the pink counters and pink floor. The pink kitchen was colored that way in honor of the Knights' cook, Miss Rose, so that she could work in a rose pink kitchen. Every day.

The Knights continued to vacation at their club every winter, until their deaths in 1936. The property was then sold to a group of investors, and in 1939, Ray T. Adams bought out all the others to become sole owner of the club. The hunt club was then renamed the Whalehead Club, but would not be used for its intended purpose. The advent of World War II meant that coasts were now areas of potential conflict. The building was leased from Adams for the duration of the war and used as a billet for coastguardsmen leaving boot camp and going to their assignments. After the war, the club returned to Adams.

Oddly, even though Adams seems to be the most successful person with the club, he is discussed much less than the Knights. Adams owned the club from 1939 until his death in 1957. He charged $50 a day for the exclusive use of his lodge, property, and hunting blinds, and he got it. At the time, geese and ducks were plentiful, and sportsmen could bag their limit by early morning, then spend the rest of the day fishing for bass in the sound water behind the club. Adams club was so successful, he even was written up in Sport Illustrated in 1957.

After Adams' passing, the property was again sold, and leased to be used as a boys' boarding school called Corolla Academy. Run by Hatcher Williams, who was also the headmaster at the Blue Ridge School in St. George, Virginia, it was an attempt to create a summer school program on the coast.The school was successful, but closed after two seasons when the property was again sold.

In the early 1960s, with the Cold War going strong, the Whalehead Club was used as a testing ground for solid fuel rocket research. The property of the club was more than just the building and the little bay for hunting boats. Five miles of land was included in the property for setting up blinds, and this large expanse was perfect for test firing rockets. The isolation of Corolla in the 1960s didn't hurt, either. So, in 1962, Atlantic Research Corporation leased the land for testing solid fuel rockets for aerospace purposes. The property proved so favorable for tests that the company bought the land in 1964. Even though the testing was supposed to be secret, the few villagers that lived nearby at the time would see the rockets being shot in the sky. Workers for the company even brought their families to stay at the club for vacations at the beach.

In 1969, with the growth of the Outer Banks as a popular tourist attraction, ARC found better testing sites for its rockets, and a downward spiral began for the Whalehead Club. A series of owners attempted to find a way to restore the land and buildings, but none came to fruition, and the building fell into serious disrepair. It wasn't until the 1990s that the land was purchased by Currituck County and money was found to begin restoration of the club. By 2002, the main house was restored and opened for tours.

Today, the Whalehead Club offers tours to visitors to the property. There are various choices for tours, from a traditional tour, self-guided tours, behind the scenes tours and tours of the boathouse as well. They also do ghost tours on Thursday evenings, and suggest that the kids stay at home for this one. Which means that if there is a ghost tour, there must be ghosts, right? Well, paranormal researchers do not know who it is, but they have said that someone is there. There are tales of people smelling cigar smoke when entering the dining room in which a portrait of Knight would hang. It was well known that Knight would enjoy a cigar in the room. There are stories of a spectral girl in the basement reaching out at people who visit the club, a haunted staircase, and the elevator going up and down for no reason. What makes it even more intriguing is that no usual event that causes a haunting ever happened there. There were no murders, no strange unexplained deaths, nothing tragic, to explain the presence of a ghost or specter. It seems the only deaths that occurred there were all those geese.

Oddity ★
It's not that strange, but it is pretty big. As fancy as the place is, one of the biggest selling points to taking a tour in the summer is that they have air conditioning.

Difficulty ★
Tours run daily, Monday through Saturday, and the ghost tour is once a week on Thursday nights. It's best to call ahead to make sure you will be able to get in on a tour, as that's a long drive if you are coming from anywhere down south of Corolla.

Duck
&
Southern Shores

Field Research Facility

Duck 36.18225° -75.75060°

Jutting out 1840 feet into the Atlantic Ocean, the Field Research Facility built by the Army Corps of Engineers is a pier and research observatory to study the ocean and coastline, including effects of erosion and storms. Established in 1977, the FRF consists not only of the long pier and building, but several unique, specialized vehicles as well that serve the facility.

The main feature of the facility is the pier. At 1,840 feet, it extends out more than a third of a mile into the Atlantic Ocean. In comparison, the new concrete version of Jennette's Pier built in Nags Head is only 1,000 feet long. The enormous reach of the pier into the ocean allows for greater study of wave height and frequency while the wave is still in deep water. The ocean floor is less affected by seasonal shifts of sand out that far, as well as the erosion that occurs closer to shore. The Pier was built over two years, finishing in 1977. Due to the harsh nature of winter waves, spring storms and summer hurricanes, the pier was built to withstand a severe bashing, with steel pilings going 50 to 60 feet into the ocean floor. At the end of the pier, it is in an average of 21 feet deep water, with the pier itself 25 feet above the water surface. It was raised that high in order to avoid being overtopped by huge waves that may rush ashore during a storm. Even so, the pier was overtopped during the 1991 Halloween storm.

One of the unique parts to the pier was that it had its own railroad, of sorts. The Sensor Insertion System was a large but precise crane that could lower objects into the water off the side of the pier. It ran on railroad tracks placed on the deck of the pier.

But that isn't the only specialized vehicle the FRF has. They have their own version of a DUCK, called a LARC, a Lighter Amphibious Resupply Cargo, which is used to drive from the main building, down to the beach, and then into the water. It is used to help ferry diving equipment and instruments out to the deep water without having to load and unload multiple times. Unlike other amphibious wheeled craft, this one has the sides between the wheels missing, creating a very low gunwale essentially, so that people and equipment don't need to be lifted to get into the water.

The most unique, and recognizable vehicle that the FRF has is the aptly named CRAB. The Coastal Research Amphibious Buggy is a giant three wheeled shore going tricycle of sorts. It stands 35 feet tall, with a triangular base of three water filled wheels that are about 27 feet apart. The ungainly thing looks like it would tip over if a small wave hit it, but at 18,000 pounds, it isn't going to fall. As a matter of fact, it was made to operate in waves up to 6 feet tall, meaning it could easily withstand all but the worst of what the Atlantic can throw at it. The CRAB is made to drive into the shore break and measure the amount of erosion or dropoff that occurs on the edge of the sea. It is particularly useful in measuring the effectiveness of beach renourishment. It can occasionally be seen being used during beach renourishment along the coast.

With all these tools, it should be obvious what the Army Corps of Engineers does at this place. Considering the large number of people who live or vacation close to the shores of the Outer Banks, as well as all across the United States, the Corps of Engineers takes very seriously the study of protecting all coastal areas. Many of their studies at the FRF are for monitoring effects from tropical storm impacts through winds and waves. Beach erosion and sand migration, where the sand goes when it leaves a particular beach, are also parts of their studies. Experiments continue at the FRF, with studies for determining flood risks, FEMA studies, and more.

Sadly, with government budget cuts, tours have stopped at the pier at the time of this writing. The pier is still visible from the beach, and you can still walk under the pier. There is no parking at the pier, and the entrance is gated. It does make a pretty unique sight, though, to see that thing sticking out so far into the Atlantic. It just might be worth the walk.

Oddity ★★

While piers are a common sight on the coast, this one is uncommonly long. When it was first built, the strong concrete structure was especially dissimilar to the organic, wooden creosoted fishing piers farther south.

Difficulty ★★★

There is no beach access to the pier from the FRF, and no access is nearby, so to see it, you may have to park and walk a while. Also, tours are only available at certain times, based on budget concerns and other government issues. If you really want to see it, maybe get a job there?

The Army Corps of Engineers builds and maintains over 2,500 different recreation sites across the country, making it the largest provider of outdoor recreation in the US.

Flat Top Cottages

Duck *(Going, going.... ?)*

36.13065° -75.72736° (Mackey Cottage)

36.13017° -75.72768° (Nixon Cottage) *demolished

36.12491° -75.72484° (Pink Perfection)

36.12413° -75.72538° (Atlantic Breezes)

36.12371° -75.72409° (Blair Cottage) *demolished

36.12251° -75.72457° (Sea Breezes)

36.11660° -75.72145° (Knight Cottage)

36.11019° -75.71712° (Graves Cottage and Dunne's Dune) *demolished

36.10706° -75.71606° (Powell Cottage)

36.10546° -75.71754° (Buckley Cottage)

36.10142° -75.71565° (Outer Banks Community Foundation)

In 1947, Frank Stick, an artist living on Roanoke Island with his family, purchased 2,600 acres of beachfront and soundside property north of Kitty Hawk with the plan of developing it into a community called Southern Shores. Quickly realizing that the properties would sell better with houses on them, Stick decided to build homes on the land, with a focus on locally sourced materials. With his artistic skills, Stick drew up plans for a simple home suitable for inexpensive construction and comfortable living on the Outer Banks during the summertime.

Due to the distant location, building supplies would be difficult to obtain, so whenever possible, local raw materials were used. Local sand was used to make concrete blocks that would be used to build the houses, and juniper trees from nearby Currituck were used for the interior walls and doors.

The houses all had the distinctive flat roof, with a large overhang. The wide roof acted as a brim for the houses, shading the walls and windows while letting less sun into the house, keeping it cool on hot days. Louvered windows let in the sea breeze to blow through the houses, since the louvers would allow for the entire window to open, maximizing the space, and could be left open during rainstorms so the houses would not get stuffy during afternoon showers or thunderstorms that snuck up on the Southern Shores coast. The simple buildings were functional, but not fancy.

As time went on, the flat top cottages became ubiquitous throughout Southern Shores, a popular and easily built home that went well with the wide open expanses of the beach and the scrub trees toward the sound side. But good things do sometimes come to an end. With development rampant, and property values going up, several of the houses and land

were sold, torn down to make way for larger homes with more rooms and features. Today, less than half of the original Flat Tops still exist, and fewer than that in their original state. Several have been converted into larger homes with pointed roofs, though a few still sit with their original design.

Today, the Flat Top Cottages are sought after by some as a classic design, worthy of being preserved. The Flat Top Preservation Society, a part of the Outer Banks Community Foundation, owns one building as offices and works to help preserve the rest. Tours are offered through an open house scheduled in the spring. The Flat Tops have dwindled in number partly because of the increase in cost of flood insurance for the properties. Due to insurance rules, many of the houses cannot be expanded on their property, so buyers often find it more economical to actually destroy the smaller houses and build entirely new and larger homes for rent, in order to recoup the sizeable investment into the beachfront property. The Flat Top Preservation Society is working to create a historic designation for the house designs, which may lead to more preservation and tax relief for the owners down the road. Until then, these significant homes will be vulnerable to loss over time.

The Flat Tops are easily seen driving down through Southern Shores, and are distinctive due to their diminutive size relative to the giant houses that came after them. Several are still available as rentals if there are people who want to experience the life of a 1950s homeowner. Visitors can see the unique layouts the houses have, the notable colors and shades

of paint that were popular throughout the decades, and the local concrete with little bits of sea shells imbedded in the houses' walls and foundations. Happily, air conditioning is a welcomed addition to the houses, though it might be just as well to get outside and enjoy the beach.

Oddity ★★
The Flat Top homes are getting more and more rare. Not all that go up for sale are bought by preservationists. The Flat Top Cottages certainly look different than most of the new houses on the beach.

Difficulty ★★★
Seeing them isn't too difficult. You pass by them on the road. But only look if you are the one not driving. Going into one is a little more difficult. The only access to many of these homes is either through rental, or doing a tour through the Preservation Society, which usually occurs in April. Don't go into the homes on your own, as they are private property.

While some of these houses, included the one photographed, have been demolished, there still are about 25 Flat Tops left in Southern Shores, including four that are designated historic landmarks. The local preservation group schedules tours and walks of homes on occasion.

Central Outer Banks

Monument to a Century of Flight

Kitty Hawk 36.09736° -75.71544°

In 2003, the Outer Banks was running headlong into the celebration of the 100 year anniversary of the Wright Brothers' first flight, done in Kill Devil Hills on December 17, 1903. The bulk of the celebration took place over several days at the Wright Brothers Monument, with pilots, astronauts, celebrities, and even a speech by President George W. Bush. On the rainy day that was the anniversary, thousands packed the hill and field to get a glimpse of John Travolta or the president, or perhaps to see Air Force One fly over. Most of these people would never know the decade of planning that went into arranging the festival.

One of the lesser seen parts of the tribute to the Wrights, and other achievements of air and space, is the Monument to a Century of Flight, located behind the Aycock Brown Welcome Center in Kitty Hawk. It consists of fourteen steel pylons placed along a spiraling path coming out from a central globe. Each pylon lists some of the great moments in aeronautical history, from the Wright brothers all the way up to the rovers on Mars.

Designed by local artist Glenn Eure, along with Hanna Jubran and Jodi Hollnagel Jubran, the monument has several interesting features. Most notably are the pylons, which look like stylized wings placed on end. The monument has the effect of looking like it is about to rise up out of the ground and take flight. The globe at the center is a depiction of what the Earth looks like from space. From the globe, a spiral path leads out toward the first pylon and onward. Walking the path will take the visitor 120 feet, a tribute to the distance Orville Wright flew on his first successful flight.

The monument is free to visit, and is always open, though the visitor's center has regular hours. Parking is located on the site, and there usually are spots available. Be sure to visit the visitor's center as well to get some information on the Outer Banks, where to stay, where to eat, where to visit. The building itself is pretty interesting in that it is a tribute to the old lifesaving stations and beach cottages that first populated the island. It also has air conditioning. Go on in.

Oddity

It is a pretty curious monument. There are several milestones among the 100 listed on the pylons that not everyone will know about. Try to walk the spiral path at the same speed as the Wright Flyer flew the same distance. It took Orville 12 seconds, at a leisurely 6.8 miles per hour.

Difficulty ★★

Yes, it is only a few steps up from the parking lot to the monument, but getting there from the road can be difficult with the rather confusing street signs and multiple entrances, especially coming from the Wright Memorial Bridge. The simple way to do it is, when everyone else is turning at the traffic light to go towards Duck, just turn the opposite way towards the visitor's center.

Covered Bridge

Kitty Hawk 36.0827° -75.73184°

North Carolina's creeks and streams have a natural beauty to them, a combination of lush verdant plant life, earthy aromas, peaceful trickling sounds of water washing over smooth stones, a coolness hinted on a hot day. Yes, a burbling creek or rushing stream is a true sight to behold.

Getting across one is another matter.

Getting across water is something people on the Outer Banks know more than a little about, and they know something or two about bridges, as well. But not many of them even know that there is a covered bridge on the Outer Banks.

Covered bridges are rare nowadays. New bridges, long or short, are usually made of more permanent stuff, concrete and metal, to make them last for decades. Though many are learning even those will not last forever. There are few covered bridges still standing in NC that were built before the turn of the 20th century, including the famous Bunker Hill Bridge in Claremont. Most covered bridges that exist now are modern designs, more for style than function, though they do usually serve to cross a stream.

A good question to ask is, "Why cover a bridge?" It turns out there is a pretty simple explanation for the cover on a covered bridge. Since bridges were made out of wood, a regular bridge would wear out fairly quickly, over ten years or so, when continually exposed to the elements. By covering a bridge, the trusses, the supports that hold the bridge, would last much longer, negating the need for constant repairs or replacement.

This may be why there is a covered bridge in Kitty Hawk. Built for Atlantic Township, a small housing development in Kitty Hawk Woods, the 32 foot bridge spans one of the several low spots that exists back in the newly developed neighborhood. Since the development is a private area, the roads must be maintained by the homeowners' association. Paying for landscaping is one thing, but having to replace an entire bridge every decade is a pretty big expense for a few houses. With a covered bridge, not only do the owners get a long lasting creek overpass, but they get a pretty nice looking, and extremely novel, landmark.

Oddity

Covered bridges are more often a sight to be seen in the mountainous regions of North Carolina. Seeing one on a barrier island is almost unheard of, until now.

Difficulty ★★

While the bridge is not just by a road, but actually part of the road, this is still a little hard to see. The one lane bridge is meant for cars, but you still need to be careful crossing it. And the bridge is technically private property. So unless you get an invite or you buy a house there, this one may have to go unseen.

Covered bridges were once known as kissing bridges, because dating couples could steal a kiss while hidden from peeking townsfolk under the cover of the bridge's walls.

Original covered bridges are now rare. The wood for the sides and walls were often stolen for use in building sheds, or torn off or defaced by vandals. And being all wood, they were often consumed by fires.

Kilroy Drawing

Kitty Hawk 36.05895° -75.68510° (Going, going... gone!)

"Kilroy was here"

The phrase popularized in World War II by American GIs has long been associated with the little guy with the long nose peeking over a fence to see what's on the other side. It seems Kilroy even made it to the beach.
During World War II, a saying by American soldiers found its way onto every wall, door, and dirty piece of glass still unbroken while soldiers marched through Europe. It was even said that GIs taking a beachhead for the first time would find the saying already chalked in as they secured the recent battlefield. Kilroy was so prevalent, it seemed, that the Nazis even thought he was some secret agent operating behind enemy lines with impunity, brazenly signing off that he had been there and the Germans didn't catch him.

The legend of Kilroy is somewhat obscure. No one can say definitely where the phrase came from. The drawing may be of British origin, a balding man sticking his nose over a fence, while the saying, "Kilroy was here," would be added by the American soldiers. The most popular history of the Kilroy phrase is that it came from an actual person, James Kilroy. James worked as an inspector at the Fore River shipyard in Quincy, Massachusetts. One of his jobs was to count rivets done by other workers in a shift. James would count to a mark made by the worker, then sign the now famous "Kilroy was here," to deter workers from erasing a chalk line and claim someone else's work as their own. When the ships were launched, unpainted on the insides, troops saw the writing, and ultimately found it to be a good omen, meaning to them that the ships had been checked to be seaworthy. Finding the ubiquitous phrase in strange places on the insides of the ships seemed funny to them, so they just carried on the tradition.

The little bald guy had his own catchphrase, it seems. During the start of the war for Britons, "Mr. Chad" would show up, looking over a wall for supplies in demand, often saying, "Wot, no...?" while asking for essentials. "Wot, no sugar?"

While Kilroy's popularity waned in the 1950s, the little guy has still popped up on walls and school kids' notebooks ever since then. He never has totally disappeared.

This Kilroy is painted on the beach road in Kitty Hawk. He is a little different than the classical Kilroy, with his nose missing and hair standing on end. He is in the northbound lane, so spotting him while driving is not too hard. It is actually rather easy to notice him as you drive up to and over the guy. The best way to see him, though, is just to walk up from the beach. There is an access walkway over the dunes that allows for an easy view  of the painted on face. And you better see him soon. He's looking a little tired.

Oddity ★★★
Graffiti and road art are not necessarily rare, but this is a pretty clever drawing to do. It is just a good thing no one got hit doing it.

Difficulty ★★★
Stopping in the road here is a seriously bad idea. Don't even think about doing it. Unfortunately, there are no accesses nearby, nor is there parking on the side roads. And the beach road is so narrow that walking on it is dangerous. Remember that there are a lot of people who either do not know where they are going, or may be looking the wrong way. There is an access .6 miles north in Kitty Hawk, with a bathhouse. Park and enjoy a nice walk on the beach to the walkway over the dunes, take a picture, and stroll back.

UPDATE The Kilroy art was paved over when the road was repaired and no longer peeks out at passersby.

Original Wright Brothers Monument

Kitty Hawk 36.06218° -75.70111°

You can't miss the Wright Brothers Monument, can you? The huge granite monument sits on top of Kill Devil Hill, with a big rotating beacon and spotlights shining at night. But what about the original Wright Brothers monument? When visitors go to the Wright Brothers Memorial in Kill Devil Hills, near where the first flights took place, they see where Orville and Wilbur worked and lived during the cold, windy fall days and nights on the barren Outer Banks. Part of the display is a shack used by the brothers to keep warm or rest while out testing their gliders and before they flew the plane. Their shack shows how the Wrights were sleeping in the rafters with just a small wood stove heater to keep them warm on those cold days. The only food they had was canned vegetables they had to heat up on the little wood stove. It must have been a harsh life. What is not revealed is that they also stayed in the cozy Kitty Hawk village while working on their gliders and testing their airplane. They stayed with the Tate family, living in their home, and probably getting some good Outer Banks seafood while inventing the airplane. The brothers would give the used cloth from their glider experiments to Mrs. Tate to make into shirts for her son. It may not have been as comfortable as their Ohio home, but it wasn't bad, either. In 1928, the residents of Kitty Hawk erected their own monument in front of the house where the brothers would stay while they built their first glider to test their ideas of flight. The marker was placed in the front lawn of what was the W.J. Tate family home. The people of Kitty Hawk planned, bought and put up their original monument on their own two years before the plans for the large monument to the south were ever realized. The big monument on Kill Devil Hill was not finished until 1932.

The original marker reads

On this spot Sept 17, 1900
Wilbur Wright Began the assembly of
The Wright Brothers' First experimental
Glider Which led to
Man's conquest of the air. Erected by Citizens of
Kitty Hawk NC
1928

Oddity

This is a wonderful little find, and a great tribute from some great people to some great brothers.

Difficulty ★

It is a little like going back in time to see a bit of the sleepy village of Kitty Hawk, before development hit the Outer Banks. Moore Shore Road is off to the left of West Kitty Hawk Road as you drive into the village.

Make sure you get out and read the back of the monument. Shhhh! It's not the real marker! The original was damaged by fire and the elements. It currently is on display at the Kitty Hawk Town Hall.

Kellogg's Big Chair

Kill Devil Hills 36.00308° -75.65091°

Kellogg Supply was started in 1946 by Gordon Kellogg over in Manteo when he sold salvaged lumber from the nearby naval base. His motto was, "Everything to build anything." Even a giant Adirondack chair.

Big Adirondack chairs have become more popular along the coast, but there aren't that many you can just go up and sit in. You may have some very, very large homeowner come out and yell at you, "Hey, get out of my chair!" Well, this one you can sit in. It's actually encouraged. Take a picture, sure. Just be careful getting up and down.

This chair is located at Kellogg's second store, on the beach in Kill Devil Hills, built in 1948. In addition to the usual things you would expect at a lumber store, shoppers can pick up a great deal of beach supplies, bug spray, regular sized chairs, umbrellas, the lot of it for spending a great week at the beach.

They definitely can sell you the lumber and paint to make your own giant chair, as plans for it are readily available. And they may even be able to make one for you themselves, if you ask nice and invite them to the party afterwards.

Oddity ★★

It's an abnormally big chair! Now if they can get you an abnormally big lemonade to go with it...

Difficulty ★

They have parking for the store right next to the building, but if you are planning on going to the beach, the access across the street fills up early in the summer. Be careful around all that traffic!

Nags Head Woods

Kill Devil Hills   35.98980° -75.66455°

Picture in your head what the Outer Banks would have looked like before people showed up on its shores. What would you see if you could view the barrier islands before Man put his print on the land? Most may picture wide, yellow-white beaches, low dunes, a bit of scraggy brush, hardened to carry its burden in the windswept salt air. Dunes and hills roll across the land, unfettered by grass. It is the land of seagulls, ghost crabs, and sandpipers. But would you also picture a maritime forest?

Nags Head Woods is a forest preserve on the sound side of the island, located in Kill Devil Hills and Nags Head. It is a unique and special

occurrence to have a forest grow up on what is mostly a sandy barrier island, a true will of nature for all the life there to survive, thrive, and be interconnected.

In 1974 the land was designated a National Natural Landmark, and in 1977, the Nature Conservancy began their work to protect the land and increase the area of the woods being protected. Through a series of donations and work with the towns involved, Nags Head Woods grew into a 1400-acre parcel that runs on the west side of Kill Devil Hills all the way south to the edge of Jockey's Ridge.

The woods are not necessarily a fluke of nature, or a piece of luck, but more an exercise in tenacity to hang on and flourish on the part of the plants and animals that live there. The reasons the woods exists are manyfold. Before the large dunes were built on the Atlantic shore in the 1930s, ocean overwash into the sound was a common occurrence. While the heavier sand was quickly deposited on the beach, the lighter silt would be lifted and carried farther, creating overwash fans on the sound side of the islands. This softer, more tightly packed loam was excellent for plant growth. In addition, just to the north of the woods was a mammoth sand dune that helped to protect the trees and other plants from the strong, bitter, salty wind that would blow in from the north, creating an, if not mild, then at least slightly less harsh environment. The benefit of fresh water pools and the less salty sound gave the plants much needed water to help them grow. As the plant life took hold, animal life found a home.

Today, Nags Head Woods is a macro environment in a microcosm. Though it is a maritime forest, it has similarities to mountain forests in its diversity. Inside the Woods exists a maritime deciduous forest of hardwoods and pines on the upper parts of dunes, a maritime swamp forest in the swales between the dunes where gum and willow trees grow, a maritime shrub forest with local brush, and interdunal ponds, low places where fresh water has gathered into pools, creating still waters that supply moisture for plants and animals along their shores.

And animals are abundant in the woods. Birds and lizards live happily in the branches and leaves throughout the forest. Snakes, frogs, and turtles are often found at the various waters' edges. Red bellied water snakes and slider turtles are just a few of the denizens of Nags Head Woods. There are venomous snakes in the woods, cottonmouths and rattlesnakes, but they usually avoid people if possible. In the numerous ponds, the swamp canary, with its yellow plumage, can often be spotted in the trees and shrubs.

Visiting Nags Head Woods is easy, with a small parking lot and over 5 miles of trails leading out of the visitor's center. The trails are unpaved and natural, but with little elevation change, they are easy to walk, as well as being shaded from summer's sun. There is a new addition to the trails, as there is now a mile long trail for people with disabilities. There is an unpaved road that runs from the visitor's center south toward Jockey's Ridge. The road is mostly sand, with some tight turns. While passable for most vehicles, (4wd is usually not needed,) the road is a tight one lane, with steep dunes on one side, and a dropoff on the other. If you meet someone going the other way, it sometimes is difficult to pass, and you better hope they are going slow.

There are other ways to see the woods. Nags Head Woods has a 5k run every Mother's Day weekend in the spring, and the sandy road is part of the Outer Banks marathon that runs from Kitty Hawk to Manteo.

While the preserve is full of natural beauty, there is a lot of history in Nags Head Woods as well. The area was not only protective for the trees, but for people as well.

In the 19th century, Nags Head Woods was home to an Outer Banks community, with homes, a church, and school. Today, there is little left to see. There are remnants of a house's foundation, and some of the old cemeteries have survived. This leads to the many legends about the area.

Vague ghost stories abound for Nags Head Woods. The remoteness and creepiness of a forest with only historical remnants to define it often invokes tales of haunts and spooks. There is one legend of a cemetery where a tree had grown into the coffin, and if you tickle the tree, the corpse will laugh, making the tree tremble and shake. The woods themselves have been the subject of legends over the decades, supposedly used by various nefarious groups for their clandestine gatherings. The stories seem to change with the years, going from secretive clubs to crazy teens to stories of witchcraft. These tales are much more likely the imagination of the narrators of the stories, and very much less based in any real truth. Visiting at night is still not a good idea, but mostly because you might get poked with a stick more so than run into a monster.

The park is open from sunrise to sunset for anyone to come visit and walk the trails. There are a few displays at the center, and occasionally there are activities for kids, tied in with the NC Aquarium. It's also a great place to get some photos that most people don't usually see coming from the Outer Banks.

Oddity ★

Nags Head Woods is a rare thing to find on the coast, continually changing, and continually beautiful.

Difficulty ★★

Turn on Ocean Acres Dr at the traffic light by McDonalds and keep going until the road turns to sand. The parking lot is on the left. But just be sure to drive carefully if you do any exploring on the old dirt road.

There are some rare plants that grow in Nag Head Woods Preserve. The water violet blooms in April and May along the ponds, and a tiny orchid blooms in early summer

Austin Fish Company Shark

Nags Head 35.96423° -75.62836°

Just a word of warning, as you read this, you will get hungry, very hungry. Ravenous even. Possibly hungry enough to go on a feeding frenzy, like a big shark would.

The Austin Fish Company is home to fresh caught seafood, and has been for over 50 years. They sell all the usual fish and shellfish, not only the local stuff, but fresh seafood from all over, such as lobster, snow and king crab legs, the works. And if you don't want to take it back to your house and cook it yourself, they will prepare it for you. Yes, they will make you a mess of clams or a big mix of steamed shrimp, lobster, and all the usual sides just so you can take it home and feed a bundle of people. The only thing you have to do is wash your hands. Probably twice - once before you eat, and once when you are done.

They even have shark on the menu. No, it's not there to eat. It's more of a mascot. Austin Fish Company has a giant Great White Shark over their building. For a long time now, the big shark has been a draw for people to stop and view, while at the same time they can pick up some fried shrimp or a tasty sandwich. The shark used to sit out in the lot of Austin's, later surrounded by a big shark cage, which was more to keep the shark in and the people out, rather than the other way around.

Does the shark look familiar? Do you hear haunting music? Well, go inside to check out an interesting story about a local fisherman. Donnie

Braddick runs a fishing boat out of Wanchese, but he used to work up north in Montauk, NY. While out on a charter, he got asked to come aboard the boat of famous shark fisherman Frank Mundus, who allegedly was the inspiration for the character of captain Quint in Jaws. Mundus had heard that there was a giant great white feeding on a dead whale, but needed someone to work a rod while he ran the boat. Braddick traded places with Mundus' tired charter, who went ashore. Braddick worked the rod and reel to catch the largest great white shark ever caught on a fishing pole, all 3,427 pounds of him. While not a true replica of that shark, the Austin shark certainly is a decent tribute.

Oddity

Shark week? Ha! This place, it's an everyday occurrence.

Difficulty ★★

Finding and seeing the shark is straightforward. Parking usually is not an issue, and they are used to people stopping to see the shark. However, be aware that traffic is an issue. If you are driving, keep your eyes on the road, not the shark! Please note that the shark is taken down after the tourist season is over and the market is closed.

Unpainted Aristocracy

Nags Head 35.95717° -75.62403°

Nags Head in the early 1800s was only a small colony of rugged and hearty Bankers, scratching out a living on the soundside shadow of Jockey's Ridge. The descendants of fishermen and the occasional shipwrecked sailor or land pirate grew up doing their best to get by, not realizing that their hardscrabble home was soon to become a tourist destination. In the 1830s, hoping to escape the stillness and heat of the mainland, families would come over on boats to the soundside port in order to enjoy the summer ocean breezes of the Outer Banks. Soon hotels were popping up, and the Bankers were making money selling vegetables to tourists, or giving them a carriage ride over to the beach on the newly built sound to sea boardwalk.

But it wasn't until 1855 that the first actual beach house was built in Nags Head. That summer, Dr. W. G. Pool purchased 50 acres of the beach from a local family for the hefty sum of $30. He built his first house there on the beach, a wonderful great shack built on stilts to let the storm driven waves wash underneath without harming the building. The house was made of mostly scavenged or local parts, as bringing in lumber meant floating the wood in on boats. The house was sided with wooden shakes or shingles, and since paint was an unavailable extravagance, the house was left in its natural wood color. But the first house was built for Dr. Pool, his wife, and his family. However, since this was the first one built on the beach, his wife was lonely as her friends still all were in Elizabeth City. So he then parceled out the other properties to their friends, selling them a plot of land for $1 each, for them to build their own beach houses.

By 1885 there were 13 houses built on the shore for 13 families to enjoy the summer ocean and sand. The houses were enlarged in the early to mid 1900s. While space was added to the homes, the style was kept, including the unpainted wooden shingles. The houses stood sentinel over decades of events, including hurricanes, the Second World War and German U-boats off the coast, and the Ash Wednesday Storm, among many things. It wasn't until the 1960s that tourism grew on the beach and started bringing more vacationers, with more motels and shops, that the

Unpainted Aristocracy finally was not alone in being a seasonal home for visitors to the Outer Banks.

Besides the unpainted wooded shingles, the houses that make up the Unpainted Aristocracy share many other characteristics, some adopted by other houses later on, with some not found on any other beach home. All the houses were built on pilings, which, when the ocean waves got tall from storms, would allow the waves to wash underneath the houses. The pilings also allowed for the houses to be lifted easily off the foundations, as they were not secured to the pilings, so that the houses could be moved back away from the approaching sea if a storm was imminent. The houses would essentially be placed on giant wheeled carts and pulled by a team of horses. When the storms had passed, the houses were simply moved back.

One of the benefits of having a house on pilings, as any kid playing at the beach knows, is that it is always cooler in the shade under the house than out in the hot sun. The underside of these beach houses would be a great place to escape the midday heat, while still being able to play in the sand. Unfortunately, kids weren't the only creatures relaxing in the coolness of the shade. Wild pigs often found their way into the shade and would rest under the houses, not only creating a worrisome pest, but also creating a terrible stink. A simple solution was created by nailing horizontal boards to the pilings, usually with a gate to allow access only to those with working thumbs. These pig fences became the style of most houses on pilings ever since.

In order to take advantage of the ocean breeze and salt air, the houses were all built with large wrapping porches, with hip roofs that more easily withstood the strong winds of storms and hurricanes. The porches would often have a built in bench to go with them, a common sitting area for the family to share. Simple push out shutters, sheets of wood hinged at the top, allowed the windows to open for fresh air, but at the same time shaded the insides from the sun throughout most of the day. The shutters could be pulled in easily, then hooked to the window frame in order protect the windowpane and the house from storm winds and the accompanied rain. This ultimately led to houses throughout the Outer Banks to be littered with what visitors might find as numerous indescribable wooden dingbats of sorts. Pieces of wood, maybe 1 inch by 2 inches and a couple of feet long, with angles cut in both ends, that were used as props to hold open the shutters, usually accompanied the windows of many a beach house for decades. Even when the big shutters became ungainly, or lost, these little sticks, paint peeling off, could be found lying in and around most older coastal houses.

One rather unique feature was found on these houses that many a kid would wish they had when they vacation on the beach. While the houses were designed to withstand wind, rain, heat, and storms though various means, sometimes a storm may come up too quickly to move the house or in any way prepare it for an ocean onslaught. If this happened, the owners would quickly pack their belongings, then open a trap door built into the floor as they left. Yes, these houses had trap doors built into the main room of each of them. While this seems like a bad idea, as the rising tide of water would clearly enter the house and flood it, that was exactly the plan. The houses, while seemingly ornate now, were merely shacks of sorts. Damage from flooding could be repaired. The danger was that if the water rose up quickly to a sealed house, the ocean could lift the house off its unsecured pilings and send it floating away, either into another home, or perhaps out to sea to be crushed by the waves. If the water entered the house, it would simply flow around the insides, just another guest enjoying a stay of sorts. When the water receded, the mess inside could simply be swept out the trap door through which it came in.

Not that the owners did all, or most of the work. They were on vacation, after all. The first families to build in Nags Head would bring their help with them to the beach for the summer. One legend in particular is tied to the Unpainted Aristocracy, that of the Seven Sisters. The story begins with seven girls or women imprisoned on a slave ship from Africa bound for the U.S. Though not truly sisters, they bonded on the voyage, promising to look after each other through the difficult times ahead. After the Civil War, though technically free from bondage, they still needed to work to earn money. The sisters had discussed either raising funds to get back home to Africa, or to set out on their own in the newly reunited U.S. They worked for the people that had owned them during slavery, traveling to Nags Head with the family to clean and cook. Once they earned enough money for whatever their decision was, be it to go back to Africa or stay in America, they immediately collected their pay and left, all seven together. No one knows what happened to them, where they went, what they decided. But the very next day a huge storm blew in to the Outer Banks, and south of Jockey's Ridge formed a new line of dunes, seven sand hills all the same size. They became known as the Seven Sisters.

That is not the only strange story associated with the Unpainted Aristocracy. Its founder, Dr. Pool, is part of a strange and sad ghost story that is retold over the years, especially when the storm winds blow on the Atlantic. Before tourism took hold on the Outer Banks, much of the local citizenry was made up of less savory characters, including people known as breakers. Breakers were essentially land pirates, people who would trick ships into beaching on the shore or sand bars at night by using lights to make the coast look more like a safe harbor. Once the ships were aground, the breakers would kill whatever crew there was and take what they

 wanted from the ship, before scuttling the craft or breaking it apart for its wood. By the 1850s, most of these breakers were long dead, but their children remained. One woman, now old and ill, offered to pay Dr. Pool for his medical services with a portrait of a woman in white that hung in the old lady's simple house. The painting made it back to Pool's home in Elizabeth City, where the portrait was identified as being of Theodosia Burr Alston, daughter of Aaron Burr, the third Vice President of the United States. Theodosia had gone missing, along with the sailing ship upon which she traveled to see her father, at the end of the year of 1812. No one truly knows of her

fate, whether she was killed at the hands of breakers, or by pirates at sea, but her portrait, possibly a gift for her father, made it to shore somehow. The entire tale of Theodosia Burr Alston, as well as her father's, is long and tragic, and seemingly doesn't end with her death, as her ghost is often rumored to walk at several of her favorite spots along the coast of the Carolinas. But that's another book.

Those are but a few of the many stories that abound in the Unpainted Aristocracy. There are plenty more from where those came. More than one house is said to be haunted, with ghostly shadows lingering in kitchen doorways, items moving, strange sounds and strange tales to go with them. And as much fun as they are, why not make your own stories by staying in one? Several of the houses are available for rent, and the location both on the beach and near Jockey's Ridge makes for a great place to stay and play. If not, even the builders of newer houses have seen the appeal of the Unpainted Aristocracy and have designed modern homes with the old Nags Head style. Who doesn't like a day at the beach?

Oddity ★

The houses are definitely different than the newer homes being built on the coast, and that's a good thing. Who needs a pool when you have the whole Atlantic Ocean?

Difficulty ★

The area is actually named the Historic District, but most long time locals know it by the more affectionate moniker. Seeing the houses is easy, as they can be seen both from the beach road, and from the shore. But remember that the houses are privately owned, even if they are for rent. The best way to see the inside is to either rent one, or get an invite from an owner.

Some of the houses of the Unpainted Aristocracy sit on open land, with no dune line. Many of the dunes that line the Outer Banks from Corolla to Ocracoke were manmade. They were projects created in the 1930s by the WPA and CCC. The thought was that without a high dune system,the unprotected islands would be essentially washed away. Little did they know that the newly made dunes actually created a larger problem of soundside erosion.

The Seven Sisters dunes disappeared in a much more public way. They were plowed down to build the Outer Banks Mall.

Jockey's Ridge Mini Golf

Nags Head 35.95764° -75.62690°

In the early 1970s, Alton Meekins was able to acquire a prime piece of real estate in the southeast corner of Jockey's Ridge, a huge attraction for visitors and their kids, and built a mini golf course on its ever shifting sands. Jockey's Ridge Mini Golf had almost everything going for it, as people could play a round of golf right in the corner front yard of the giant dunes. Not only that, the theme of the place was incredibly enticing for kids. A giant pirate ship sailed on the waves of sand, its prow sticking out into the parking lot, a visual "Stop Here!" screaming at kids to get them screaming at their parents. The ship was manned by a pretty scurvy crew, obvious by the figures on the deck, a pirate forcing a blindfolded sailor to walk the plank over the entrance to the ship, while another buccaneer was on lookout in the rigging. In addition, a friendly yellow-green octopus sat in the dunes nearby, its tentacles up like it was waving at cars as they drove by.

Customers entered through the hull of the ship, which held within it not the usual pirate's booty, but the cashier where the clubs and golf balls were handed out. It also included a small arcade of pinball machines and the new video games that would eat your quarter with ease. Once through the pirate ship, there were two 18 hole courses from which to choose, with the rather unique and flashy décor that always went with a mini golf course. A giant cobra head reared up on one hole, and a big dragon lashed out its tongue on another. The huge pink sea shell probably sent kids to wondering if they got to knock their golf ball into it, sending their ball caroming around until it made it to the hole. But all those attractions were just secondary to the big question. Which course had the castle? That was the one everybody wanted to play.

The castle was as much a landmark as anything on the property, a huge building where players actually entered to putt. The building was large by mini golf standards, where usually even windmills were rather diminutive. This castle was big enough to stand in, and probably big enough to park a small car in, if a car could ever make it through all that sand.

And that was the problem, all that sand. Jockey's Ridge was, and is, constantly migrating. At the time of building Jockey's Ridge Mini Golf, its namesake was actually moving east, toward the two lane by-pass. Dump trucks would constantly be filled with sand from the dune to keep the road clear, and then go dump the sand in the back of the ridge, where it would again continue its migration. Unfortunately for the mini golf course, the sand changed its track, and started moving south. The course's first 18 holes were actually covered over, and a new set of holes was built on the far south end of the property. At the same time, the parking lot started getting covered, to the point that a bulldozer had to be employed to uncover the spaces. Even with all the work, Jockey's Ridge Mini Golf couldn't keep up with the inevitable.

By 1987, the property was being routinely covered by sand, even though it was still in use. Sometimes players would have to putt through sandtraps that formed naturally on the artificial green grass of the holes. It was finally taken over by the state and abandoned by the owners. There was still value in the property, as the ship, which was actually built as a ship by a shipbuilding firm, was moved south to where Nags Head Church is today, where it was used as a youth hall. The octopus was dismantled and moved over to the causeway in Nags Head, where it sat for several years. Most of the golf course was dismantled and removed, including the cobra and the dragon, as well as some of the concrete foundations for the greens. But the castle was too big. The castle stayed.

It remained on site, a sturdy construction of cement and rebar, and became a popular spot to visit when people walked over to Jockey's Ridge. But even the castle couldn't withstand the flow of sand. Soon, it became embedded in the sand, and then covered until only the turrets stood above the dune line. Occasionally, on windy winter days, the sand got blown out at just the right way for the castle to be uncovered. This was a treat to many, as people would often visit and photograph the aging castle. Others, however, took the time to vandalize it, spray painting the insides with less than family friendly markings. The park service ultimately put up a fence around the castle, less a barrier and more a gentle nudge not to get too close. The castle had seen its best days, and the rebar would randomly stick out, a near silent warning, where the wind blows through and whispers, "tetanus..."

The castle becomes covered and uncovered over the years, depending on the whims of the wind. It is blocked off by sand fences and netting, with

 good reason. The rebar and broken walls that promote injury if explored. The holes were mostly removed, but a few of them were left, with bits of concrete and green carpet grass to mark them if the winds uncover the remains. No, you can't play it now; the hole is long gone, along with the rest of the course. But if you stop for a moment, close your eyes and pretend, you can go back to that time, the two lane road, a cold root beer, those soft, bouncy, colored balls, a smile from your father as he lets you go first, the joy of the first putt, the dance you do on your toes when you get a hole in one...

Oddity ★★

When it was first built, people were amazed that someone could actually buy a piece of Jockey's Ridge. Now there is little left. But if the castle ever gets uncovered, it is a true sight to behold.

Difficulty ★★★★

"What?!" you say. "It's just off the road!" Yes, it is. But here's the problem. People can and do park across the street at Kitty Hawk Kites and walk over, right to where the castle is. But if they took the time, they would notice the big sign that says the Park Service recommends parking at their lot on the north side of the dune, about a mile away, and that people cross at their own risk. Yes, there is a light, but that doesn't stop a car. Why do you think the light was put there in the first place? Also, sand spurs. If you aren't familiar with these little weeds of the devil, you will be. You... will... be. Thick soled, closed toed shoes and long pants and jeans will help, but not totally protect you from these guys if you go wandering too far afield. Don't think you'll be safe in flip flops and shorts.

The pirates on the ship were rather creepy figures. Pity the poor guy being forced to walk the plank, with his hands tied and blindfolded. One can only imagine how many kids were terrified of these mannequins and their deadly game. Unfortunately for the pirates, in the 70s there was much mischief in stealing golf course decor, including the pirates, as well as a tiger and gorilla from the African themed World Wide Golf up the road. Usually those figures ended up not far from the courses, as the thieves realized that not only did they not really have a plan to keep the figures, but they were also very heavy!

Stinson Ranch

Nags Head 35.94596° -75.62943°

Stinson Ranch was a small, old, soundside shack built on the Roanoke Sound back around 1903, as a part of several waterside houses that once existed by the shallow waters of Nags Head's western shoreline. The house was purchased by the Stinson family in 1963, and over the years became not only the iconic second home for a family to use as an escape to the idyllic life on the Outer Banks, but also a symbol to others as a sign of simpler times, of what real vacation looked like, of what many a local and visitor knew of as what was best in life.

The sound front of Nags Head is now just a little old road, a few old houses, a few new ones, and a small beach that often gets crowded with tourists bringing their kids out to the safe shallow waters of Roanoke Sound. But over 100 years ago, this was the center of life in old Nags Head. Not only was this where boats would dock, but this was where the locals would live. There were no roads, no bridges to get to the islands, and the sound offered not only travel access, but the ability to eke out a living by fishing on these waters. The waters of the sound were far off from where they are now, maybe 100 yards, maybe much more. Stinson Ranch, before it was known as such, was built on a sandy patch, lot 18 of 29 that stretched far off into what is now Roanoke Sound. It is unknown exactly when the shack was built, but its provenance can be traced back to 1903.

The house had several owners over the succeeding years, and each probably watched as the waterfront crept closer and closer to the house. In 1963, the house was bought by the Stinson family, and earned its now well known name, the Stinson Ranch. The Stinsons collected all the flotsam that came up to the house, old buoys, floats, crab pots, the bits and pieces of life on the sound. The detritus of the sound became the decorations of the house. The Stinson Ranch stood for years, fighting and winning against storms, hurricanes, tornadoes, and high waves. The Stinson family used the house as an escape, a place to rest as well as to recreate family closeness. The family used the house for birthdays, wedding celebrations, and an annual New Year's party. Every December 31st, the Stinsons would write their regrets of the past year on pieces of paper, then place the papers on a boat, and set the boat out onto the sound with a lit candle on it. The candle would burn down and set the boat aflame, sending all their regrets, now ashes, to the wind and water. When asked if the remnants of a boat would ever float back, Billy Stinson had a beautiful, and apropos, answer. "Everything eventually returns."

This would become especially meaningful on August 27, 2011, when Hurricane Irene cut a most dreaded plot through the Outer Banks, sucking the water out of the sound, and then unleashing it all, flooding the homes on the normally peaceful sound side of the islands. Many houses were flooded; roads were covered with water and debris. But the Stinson Ranch did not survive the onslaught. The house was removed, wiped clean off its pilings, lost to the rage of the storm. All that was left of the house were a few stair steps, leading nowhere.

But true to Billy Stinson's words, "Everything eventually returns," the Stinson ranch has been rebuilt. It looks the same, pretty much. The house sits on the same footprint, still a wood shingled shack hanging over the water with a walkway to the road. It doesn't yet have the patina of age, nor is it festooned with the decorations of its predecessor. But those things will come, with time. Everything returns.

Oddity ★★

A house over water is a beautiful sight, and this house is incredibly unique.

Difficulty ★

Found at the end of a dead end road behind Jockey's Ridge, Stinson Ranch is private property and there is no public parking. Many people visit to take pictures, and temporary parking is okay along the road. Go before dusk, as the road is popular with photographers and visitors to view the sunset over the sound.

When the large protective dunes were built on the beach side of the Outer Banks, they were thought to serve two purposes; first, to provide much needed employment during the 1930s, and also to protect what was seen as a fragile coastline quickly being denuded of plant life that held the sandy island together. What really happened was that all of the ocean overwash was ended, and the silty sand that helped build the soundside part of the Outer Banks was cut off. This caused massive erosion on the western side of the barrier islands, which is partly why the land where Stinson Ranch now sits is under water.

Jennette's Pier Shark

Nags Head 35.91005° -75.59546° (Going, going,... gone!)

The current Jennette's Pier is an all new pier and building that shares only the same footprint with the last building that sat on Nags Head's beach. It may be fitting that the only thing the new and old piers share is the land, because the land is probably the most historical part of the whole area.

The first Jennette's Pier was built in 1939 by Warren Jennette and was the first pier built on the Outer Banks. The land upon which it sat originally was a transient work camp, where workers stayed in cabins while they built the manmade sand dunes to protect the islands from the regular overwash of storms and hurricanes. Jennette and his family purchased the land and hired a company to come drive the pilings into the sand off the coast. By July 1939 the pier stuck 754 feet out into the Atlantic Ocean. The cabins that once held workers now were temporary homes for fishermen who came out to fish on the new Jennette's Pier. One cabin was even moved to the entrance of the pier to sell food and drinks.

For 60 years, Jennette's Pier stood as the patriarch of fishing piers on the Outer Banks. Not only was it the gathering place for anglers, its location at Whalebone Junction, the point where the beach roads would split to go to Manteo or Hatteras, meant that this beach was the nearest access for Roanoke Island residents, especially the local kids from Manteo. Thus Jennette's became a hangout, and its name became synonymous with the entire beach area for the high school students that made the spot their home for the summer.

Jennette's Pier stood against the storms, the hurricanes, and all the weather that was thrown at it for decades. Occasionally repaired, as well as enlarged, Jennette's lasted under the love and care of the family that owned it. The pierhouse was replaced with a much larger building, adding a restaurant and an arcade. The pier changed hands over time, ultimately ending up sold to the NC Aquarium in 2003 to be used as an educational research facility and an outreach for the aquarium in Roanoke Island. Nature took a hand in the pier that same year, as Hurricane Isabel rolled into the Outer Banks, and snapped off most of the pier, taking the heavy timbers to the deep.

But all was not lost. The NC Aquarium decided to rebuild the pier, only with an even bigger sense of permanence. The pier would be 1000 feet long, and built of concrete. This pier would reach out into the ocean farther than the original, or any other fishing pier on the Outer Banks. It still would retain a classic look, with a wooden walkway and railings, but the pier would be all new. It also would sport a few new designs on it. Most noticeably would be the three wind turbines that stick up from the pier and provide about half the power that the pier needs. The pier also has solar panels that charge batteries to power the pier's lights at night, and deep wells that are used to regulate the temperature of the building passively. In addition, old technology of rainwater cisterns is used to collect the rain to be used for washing the decks and the aquarium's vehicles. The pier has been certified as LEED Platinum by the Green Building Council.

Little is left of the original pier. The current Jennette's Pier does sit on the same footprint as the old pier, but nothing is left of the old building. There is a bit of the old scales used to weigh any large fish caught at the old pier, but they are not on display. The closest things left from the old pier are a few displays from the aquarium that were displayed at the original pier. On the south side of the pier is a shark done up by taxidermists as a representation of the largest mako shark ever caught in North Carolina, as well as a sailfish on display above the outside storerooms. The original mako was caught in 1983, by Russ Langford of Great Falls, Va. The 768 pound beast was pulled aboard Captain Tony Tillett's charter boat, the *Carolinian*.

Even the beach has changed over the years. Due to the ongoing erosion from strong Atlantic waves, Nags Head began beach renourishment of their coast. While the soft natural yellow sand of times past is now gone, the Jennette's Pier beach is now a long, wide, white sand stretch of beach, great for families with little kids, still a nice location for teenagers coming over from Roanoke Island, and a good spot to go for a swim in the summer.

And, of course, it is still a great place to cast a line.

Oddity  There are a few neat little things to find on the pier. Not only does it have the shark and sailfish there is also a giant turtle and a pelican somewhere on the pier. On the steps to the upstairs greatroom and deck there is also some other record catch fish, but this can only be seen if the upstairs is not being used for a private event. The aquarium also has some fish in large tanks on display in the pierhouse.

Difficulty

Sure, it is right off the road, everyone can find it. Those big wind turbines can be seen for miles. But what makes the pier so nice also makes it popular. This is a difficult place to find a spot to park during the summer, even with the two large parking lots on either side of the beach road. Go early in the day during the summer. There is a suggested donation to walk out on the pier, and a fee if you want to fish.

Update The shark took a tumble in a windstorm, and was damaged in the fall. It was removed and replaced with a swordfish. There is also a large sailfish, marlin, and other world or state records around the pier.

During the summer, when the water is clear, rays and other schooling fish are easily seen, along with the few remains of the old pier's pilings. The pier also has several locations with signs showing how it is saving water and energy to be a greener facility.

Whalebone Junction

Nags Head 35.90756° -75.59736°

Visitors driving from the North Outer Banks either to Roanoke Island or towards the Hatteras seashore are bound to pass by a little spot with a curious name. While still part of Nags Head, it is always referred to as Whalebone Junction. This conglomeration of roads, where Highway 158, the Beach Road, Old Oregon Inlet Road, Highway 64 and Highway 12 from Hatteras meet, actually got its name quite honestly. While many towns and places on the Outer Banks have strange roots, Whalebone Junction was simply named that because there were whale bones there. How they got there is a little more complex.

In the 1930s, a large dead whale had washed up during an extremely high tide down on the beach near Pea Island. Its corpse was caught in the low scrubby dunes, but with few people down to see it, or smell it, the whale was left to rot. About a year later, Alexander Midgett loaded the mostly bony carcass on the back of his truck, took the ferry across Oregon Inlet, and brought the whale's remains to Nags Head. He and his son Charles scrubbed the bones clean to make them nice and white, as well as to remove the natural aroma of dead whale. Then the bones were put up on display across the street from Midgett's gas station, naming the place "Whale Bone Service Station." The intact skeleton, displayed on spikes as a spectral whale swimming in the air, attracted plenty of onlookers to the service station, and served as free advertising for years.

The bones, along with the earliest gas station, are now long gone. The original station burned down in the 1940s, and a few bones seem to have popped up around there every once in a while. A rib or a vertebra might have been out for people to see, just to give credence to the name, perhaps. But the whale itself has moved on to other waters, it seems.

Oddity★★★

This was an important area in the early 1900s, as it was the closest place many people could get to a road if they came from the south. This is where the kids living at Bodie Island Light caught the bus to school. Now it is a good spot to pick up a cold drink from the 7-11, or a burger from Dune Burger. They do'em their way.

Difficulty ★★

Yes, the bones are gone, so there is nothing to see, right? Well, keep your eyes open anyway. It really is a junction, where essentially five roads meet up, with a lot of people not knowing where they are going.

Some people say that the bones were moved over to the aquarium in Manteo. While there are whale bones there on a nature path near the sound, the bones came from NOAA. They were probably confiscated and given to the aquarium for educational purposes.
See them at 35.91764° -75.70518°.

The Causeway

A Did You See That? Detour

Traveling the strip of road from the Nags Head beaches towards Manteo, Wanchese, and Roanoke Island, people often enjoy the view of looking out to either side of the road and seeing only water and reedy, marshy islands, uninhabited except for the birds that wade in the shallows. Rarely would they think to look down, to look straight forward, and realize just how narrow that land they travel is. The causeway that connects the barrier islands and Roanoke Island is a tiny, low strip of land that runs through a few marshy spots, with a tall bridge to let the fishing boats get out to the Gulf Stream.

The causeway originally seemed too small to support much in the way of business. With only a few restaurants, a little motel, a shell shop, and a tiny fresh seafood market, the causeway was just the right mix of unique and barren. Most people driving by these places and over that road would not realize just how old that road really is.

The causeway, the thin land bridge that connects the beaches and Roanoke Island, was made long ago by the detritus of local aboriginal groups that lived along the coast. The Hatterask and Croatan native tribes that lived along what is the modern day Outer Banks were typical of hunting and fishing tribes as they gathered their food off the land. Or in their case, the water. While hunting for game was prevalent, fishing was much more successful for most coastal tribes. They not only caught fish in the sound using nets and traps, they also fed themselves from oyster beds. Oysters were actually the third most prevalent food source for island natives over several hundred years of habitation. One of the by-products of eating lots of oysters, as well as the natural growth of oysters in the fresh waters of the sound, is oyster shells. Natives would create gigantic shell beds of oysters over the centuries all across the islands. It is likely that later inhabitants then used the excess of shells to slowly pile up a land bridge to allow them to travel more easily from the beach islands to the more wooded Roanoke Island to the inland.

While most believe that natives created the land bridge, it more likely that they traveled by boat to Roanoke Island. But it is understandable to see why people would think that. Roanoke offered lots that the beach lacked. It was relatively sheltered from the storms that would pound the coast, as well as offering a greater number of animals to hunt, especially deer, which found Roanoke Island easy to access from the mainland. Roanoke Island also offered more natural resources and easier use of nets for fishing.

The causeway has grown and changed over the years, but there are still things to see, and places to visit. While The Oasis, a restaurant famous for its lace cornbread served by barefoot college coeds, has been replaced by condos that share its name, people can still stop by The Shipwreck. The Shipwreck has been a required stop off when coming to and from the beach for decades. Yes, it sells the usual gifts, novelties, seashells, and a little of everything else. The building hasn't changed in decades, with its big front windows showing off all that is inside. Out front, an old boat painted silver offered up driftwood. Earlier in its life, The Shipwreck had a similar spot out back held large turtles swimming in a tank. Many times in the past kids would ask to stop by The Shipwreck to see the turtles.

Just to the west of The Shipwreck, just off the bridge, sits a tiny seafood market building with a big logo. Midgett's Seafood is easily recognizable with its giant crab painted on the roof. Midgett's seems to sit at the end of the road, a barrier to keep people from driving into the sound. Originally, Midgett's had a prime spot, as the bridge to Manteo used to cross right next to the market. The old bridge was replaced by a new bridge in the 1980s. Now Midgett's is slowly falling down. *Update* The Midgett's Seafood building is now gone, lost to time as it fell in on itself.

Progress has changed the causeway. In addition to the new bridge, new houses, condos, and a big marina have all been built. Restaurants were torn down, new restaurants were built. No, you can't be served by barefoot college coeds anymore, but you can still get great fresh local seafood. The Lone Cedar was built on the causeway and quickly became a hit with locals and visitors alike. While many restaurants use frozen seafood, caught and frozen in other countries, Lone Cedar only serves local fresh seafood. If it isn't caught here, it isn't served there.

Yes, things change. Progress, growth, for good or bad, will be happening. But it is good to know that there is still a bit of impressive history, right beneath our feet.

A nice little hidden spot along the causeway can be found under the long bridge. The traffic light just past the big bridge is mainly used for access to the marina. But turn the other way and you can drive to a boat ramp and dock that sits directly under the bridge.

Roanoke Island and Dare Mainland

Shad Boats

Manteo 35.90841° -75.66939°

For a sleepy little town like Manteo, there sure are a lot of things to do in the downtown. It may look like Mayberry, with its one theater and old courthouse, not to mention that America's most famous sheriff lived in the town for much of his life, but don't be fooled, this is a happening place. There are cafés, pubs, fine dining, and sandwich shops to get something to eat, and stores that sell a bit of everything. The old courthouse is now home to the Dare County Arts Council, with local art on display and for sale. You can even go over to the old Fearing hardware store to take a class in working a loom, at Endless Possibilities, a local non-profit organization for Dare County.

The downtown formed around Shallowbag Bay, where nowadays visitors might see kayaks, sloops, giant ocean going yachts, and anything in between. There are plenty of choices for the sightseer to take a trip out onto the sound. Kids can do a pirate themed ride, while adults can find a leisurely pontoon boat cruise or a fishing trip. But the most unique experience is going to be found over at the George Washington Creef Boathouse. Part of the Roanoke Island Maritime Museum, the Creef

Boathouse is part museum, part boating school. Inside are several examples of the different types of boats that once sliced through the bay, from rowboats and sailboats to a tiny speedboat. The boathouse offers classes on boatbuilding, knot tying, and youth sailing. They even have a class where a group of four can work together to build a working rowboat.

For those less interested in classes, the boathouse also offers a very unique experience, a ride in the state boat of North Carolina, the shad boat. Every Tuesday evening, weather permitting, skilled sailors take guests out for a ride in a replica of the original shallow draft fishing boats that local watermen used long ago to ply the waves along Roanoke Island. It is a wonderful way to experience the island from a different point of view. After boarding the boat, guests simply sail away from the dock. If it is a windy evening, the wind will quickly die down as the sail catches up with the speed of the breeze. The boat leans over slightly, and the riders can dangle their fingers in the water if it gets close enough, while the sun sets over the Manteo waterfront.

The ride is more than just relaxing, it is educational, too. The crew will happily talk about the different fishing techniques used in the local waters, from the island natives up to the fishermen who used a very similar boat to the one they sail today. Guests get to see how the sailboat works, how to tack and read the wind. Any of the people on the boat can even take a turn at steering it by handling the rudder. Other boats pass by, people who paid to ride on a big powered craft, and see the lithe little shad boat cutting its way through the sound, going wherever it wants, with happy smiling people relaxing in the breeze.

Whether before your ride or after, be sure to check out the other boats around the boathouse, including the 1883 *Ella View*. There are several boats on display inside and out. After the sail, you may even want one of your own.

Rides happen every Tuesday evening, at 6 pm. If there is a large number of people for this sail, then they will do a second sail around 7 pm as well. Riders will need to arrive early enough to sign a waiver, and get their life jackets. Even little kids as young as two can go on, and the ride is incredibly safe. The shad boat may lean a little in the wind, but it cannot tip over, due to the shape of the sail. No one has fallen off the boat, but if anyone did, the first thing they should do is stand up. Outside of the channel, the water is only 3 to 5 feet deep in most places.

Oddity

Words cannot truly express the simple joy of sailing along under the power of a summer's evening breeze.

Difficulty ★★

There can be up to two sails each Tuesday evening, if there is a large group at the 6 pm trip. It would be rare for both sails to fill up, but it could happen, so get there around 15 minutes early in order to sign the waiver There is usually enough street parking somewhere downtown, and people can walk pretty much anywhere. Sails happen through the summer up until late September.

Nearby is the Roanoke Island Marshes Lighthouse with its fourth order Fresnel lens. Just at the beginning of the pier to the lighthouse is the Manteo Weather Tower, which is used to signal mariners changes in the weather. It also has markers on it to show the water levels that were reached in Manteo during the floods from past hurricanes. Something else Mayberry never had.

Mother Vineyard

Manteo   35.92501° -75.66853°

With Roanoke Island being the home of the first English colony in the New World, it wouldn't be surprising to find that some of oldest organized farming would have happened in this area as well. What may be more surprising is that, while the Lost Colony was not really "lost" at all, there is a little mystery around the old vine that grows on Mother Vineyard Road in Manteo.

Most visitors know of Sir Walter Raleigh's financing of expeditions to the New World; it's part of the varied lore of the Outer Banks. First came a group of men, too small and unprepared to actually make a go of a colony. But a second attempt was made, with men and women, families, children, and supplies. The colonists were surprised to find that much of the land was already being farmed and used by local natives. The big question has become whether or not the colonists planted grape vines as well as other foods. Would they have done so, a labor intensive task of organizing and caring for a vineyard, when they desperately needed more essential foodstuffs and supplies?

The Mother Vineyard is a local grape, the Scuppernong. It grows easily in the wild all across the east coast. However, this vine obviously was planted by someone who meant it to be a part of an organized farm. The vine's roots are evenly spaced and have been tended in the past. They did not grow in the wild into this organized vineyard. While many people have believed that the vineyard was planted and tended by the English colonists as a way to grow grapes and make wine, others believe that the vines were planted by local natives on the island as a way to more easily harvest grapes. Indeed, this belief is backed up by evidence that not only did the natives use various modern methods of farming, such as using fish heads for fertilizing their fields, but also that they used scaffolding to shelter their plants, which would have been done both for building a trellis for a grape vine as well as to protect other plants from harsh weather. In addition, colonists noted that the natives were able to make a wine from the local Scuppernong grape. So it is very possible that Mother Vineyard actually was planted by an aboriginal tribe before the colonists arrived on Roanoke

Island.

To further confuse people, there have been many other claims on the vine.

Mother Vineyard has been claimed to be the oldest grape vine in North Carolina, as well as in the US, and the world. It is also claimed to be the source for all the scuppernong grapes that came after it. However, a horticulturalist named F.C. Reimer stated that he found older vines in Tyrrell County, and since the Mother Vineyard was obviously planted, it is more likely that the Mother Vineyard came from other wild vines, rather than being the source for all the tangled vines that came after it. Some have even said that the vines are old, but not ancient. They may have been planted as late as the 1800s.

In the end, it doesn't matter exactly how old the vine is, or who planted it. The mere fact that it exists makes it a rather cool landmark, and controversy always helps with interest. The Mother Vineyard is still growing. The Scuppernong has been named the state fruit, and clippings of the vine have been grown in other parts of the state. While the vine is a little too small to grow enough grapes to make wine in bulk, its clippings are now being grown

to create a large enough supply for Duplin Winery in Rose Hill, NC, to make a wine from grapes that are, essentially, from the vine, at least in spirit.

The vine grows on the sound side of Roanoke Island on Mother Vineyard Road. It was cut back from about 2 acres to a more manageable half an acre in the 1950s when the land was developed for a home for the

property's owners, Jack and Estelle Wilson. The vine is on private property, but can be seen easily from the road. If the leaves are not too large, the enormous root system can be seen. Jack Wilson originally didn't take to the vine's historical significance, and wasn't too keen on people walking around his property checking out the vine, and occasionally peeping in his windows, but he has grown to accept the importance of the vineyard, as well as people's fascination with it. The vine took a hit several years ago, when it was sprayed with an herbicide that started to kill parts of the plant, but with a lot of help, fertilizer, and water, the vine survived and thrived. Now sightseers can drive by any time to see the first grape vine in the New World.

Oddity ★★

Scuppernong grapes are delicious, if you know how to eat them. Pinch one end to push the juicy insides out of the skin, and suck them off the rather large seed. Don't eat the seed, and especially don't eat the skin. It is incredibly dry.

Difficulty ★

To find the Mother Vineyard, simply drive on Mother Vineyard Road. Drive through Manteo, past the high school, and turn on to Mother Vineyard Road. The road curves as it meets the sound, and the vineyard will be on the waterside, partially hidden by a hedge. It sits on private property, and while the owners understand the occasional visitor wanting to see the vine, it may be best to just view from the street.

Mother Vineyard Road loops around a large housing development. One road turned into an unpaved private drive, and many people would turn down this road, looking for the vine. So many cars went down the road that a sign was put up by the residents telling people that they missed the vine.

Elizabethan Gardens

Manteo 35.93753° -75.71128°

When great and powerful people get together to do something, amazing things often happen. When good fortune pays a visit, unique things appear. When the two mix, you get a one of a kind place like the Elizabethan Gardens on Roanoke Island.

In 1950, after visiting The Lost Colony, a select group of people came up with approaching the Garden Club of North Carolina with the idea of creating a two acre garden on nearby land as a tribute to Sir Walter Raleigh's colonists. They were Ruth Coltrane Cannon, a writer and playwright famous for her detailed novels of the Carolinas and wife of noted North Carolina philanthropist and textile magnate Charles Cannon, and Sir John Evelyn Leslie Wrench, who was the founder of the English-Speaking Union, a charity group empowered to bring together people of different languages and cultures for mutual understanding, along with his wife, Lady Hylda Henrietta Brooke Wrench. These people envisioned a garden that would represent what a traditional English garden would have looked like if the colony had succeeded, and had used New World plants and trees.

At the same time, E.W. Reinecke, a contractor, was working in Thomasville, Georgia removing some ancient statuary and stonework from the home of Ambassador John Hay Whitney, U.S. Ambassador to the Court of St. James. The statuary consisted of several statues, an Italian pool and fountain, and a marble wellhead. Reinecke mentioned to the Garden Club that they should try to acquire the statuary for use in the garden, as Whitney was planning to donate the stonework to the Metropolitan Museum. The Garden Club contacted the landscape firm of Innocenti & Webel, who were able to help acquire the statuary and begin the design of the gardens. With all the additions to the gardens, it was quickly realized that the original plans had to be changed to a much larger design to accommodate all the "new" additions.

The Elizabethan Gardens did not just benefit from all this fortunate happenstance. They also share several unique anniversaries with other events tied into the gardens. The Gardens were begun on June 2, 1953, which was also the date Elizabeth II was crowned Queen of England. The Gardens were opened on August 18, 1960, the anniversary of Virginia Dare's birth, the first English child born in the New World.

Today the Elizabethan Gardens are a wonderful place to visit. They consist of several different styles of gardens, with nice soft walkways and shaded paths. Flowers are planted to be in bloom throughout much of the year, and there is always something to see. But in noticing all of the flora, visitors may miss out on some unknown bits of history in the Gardens. The plants are only part of the story.

Guests will enter the Gardens through the gate house, a tiny gift shop and ticket office that leads to the courtyard and beyond. But stop for a moment at the gatehouse. It is a replica of a 1500s orangery, a part of a greenhouse where citrus plants would winter to protect them from the English cold weather. Above the entrance to the gatehouse is the coat of arms of Elizabeth I. Next to the gatehouse is a wrought iron gate. It is not usually used as an entrance, as people would come inside the gatehouse to pay their fee. The gate is actually a gift from the French Embassy to the U.S.

A new addition to the Gardens is the metal sculpture of Elizabeth I. This bronze sculpture is 9 feet tall, about 1 and ½ times life size, and is considered the largest bronze statue of Elizabeth I in the world. Created by sculptor Jon Hain, it was dedicated in 2006.

And that's not the only statue in the Gardens. Further along is a marble statue of Virginia Dare, envisioned as a young lady who survived into adulthood, dressed as a native princess. Her story is so intriguing, the statue gets its own chapter in this book.

The statuary gifted to the Gardens resides in a sunken garden as a center point to the site. Walking down into the formal area, visitors will see not only the various flowers in the garden, but the large Italian fountain and pool, along with its balustrade. Carved on it is the coat of arms of the Farnese family. One of the more famous members of this family was Pope Paul III. Since the fountains are dated to a time before Elizabeth I, it is likely that Pope Paul III probably walked around this very same fountain at some time in his life. The statues that are part of the sunken garden include representations of Apollo, Jupiter, Venus, and Diana. A curious recent discovery is that the Farnese family were benefactors of a famous sculptor in Italy at the time. Michelangelo or a student of his may have had a hand in the sculptures seen at the Gardens.

Just to the east of the sunken gardens are great views of the Roanoke Sound. Looking out over the water, a visitor gets an idea of what the colonists might have seen when they first settled on the island. Walking the paths through the sand is like putting yourself in the same place as Virginia Dare as a child, playing in the trees and on the beach, or where John White might have stood to ponder their fate, or maybe where Ananias Dare hunted for food for the colonists. The view was so appealing that the Gardens built a gazebo there in 1981. The gazebo is a nice place to sit and enjoy a restful moment while enjoying the view over the sound, but look closer and some discoveries about it can be made. To fit in with the rest of the gardens, as an idea of what it would have looked like had the colony flourished, the gazebo was build to be period correct. The wood is hand hewn, and joined together without any modern tools or nails. Wattle and daub, an ancient building technique that uses interwoven rods or twigs with a clay binder, is used to create the walls. The roof is made from Norfolk thatch, imported from Norfolk, England, and will last for decades.

Farther into the Gardens is the Woodland Garden. It is much less formal, with the idea being to show off native plants in their natural environment. There is nothing proper or organized like the rest of the gardens. It is a very quiet, shaded and restful spot to take a break along the walk. Look for hidden pools with swimming goldfish veiled by grass and roots.

The most decorative, as well as fragrant part of the Elizabethan Gardens is the Queen's Rose Garden, a cloistered area with numerous roses growing throughout. Be sure to check out that sundial in the rose garden. The base is over 500 years old, and part of the same collection that brought the fountain in the sunken garden from the Whitney collection. Search through the names of the various roses to find a special one. The Queen Elizabeth Rose was donated by Windsor Castle to the Elizabethan Gardens on its 25th anniversary. And since the rose garden is dedicated to Queen Elizabeth II, there even is an elevated platform for a simple throne.

Not only is Queen Elizabeth II well represented in the Elizabethan Gardens, Queen Elizabeth I has received some recent notoriety due to a discovery of a royal portrait at the Elizabethan Gardens. Discovery may be an unfair use of the word, because for 50 years the painting hung in the gatehouse for all to see. As speculation about the provenance of the painting grew, it gained attention from specialists in the field, even appearing on the television show Treasure Detectives. The portrait was purchased from a New York art dealer in the 1950s by Ruth Coltrane Cannon, who thought a painting of the queen should grace the gardens. It is likely that she never thought about how old the painting was. Or even the uniqueness of the portrait. The painting shows a depiction of an aging, wrinkled, yet still stern and powerful queen. A depiction that would have never been approved by the royal court. The queen would never want to have herself been shown as a person not long for the world, a ruler who may not have the strength to rule. No one can be sure how the painting was created, whether the artist kept the painting hidden, or how it escaped royal censors. In modern times it probably was not even noted to be contemporary to the time of Elizabeth I. But it is. Probably. The painting is attributed to a famous portrait artist, Marcus Gheeraerts the Younger. It shares many similarities with another portrait of Elizabeth I done at his studio at the same time period as this one. It could be that the two portraits were done simultaneously, or that this one was a practice or study piece. No one will know why it was created, but it most likely is a legitimate portrait of the queen, and possibly the only one that shows her comfortable in her age.

When the picture was discovered to be so rare and valuable, it was taken down, conserved and stored in a more appropriate location. It later went on tour, being displayed for the first time since its sale outside of North Carolina at the Folger Shakespeare Library in Washington, D.C. It has also made appearances in other museums, including the Museum of the Albemarle in Elizabeth City. A replica is now on display in the gatehouse.

All of these facts, all of the history of the Elizabethan Gardens, certainly help give the place a more detailed chronicle of its life, but visitors must realize that the real life of the gardens is in the plants, the flowers, the trees. Go and enjoy the blooms, the leafy canopy, find the flowers you like. Walk in the path that maybe Sir Richard Grenville walked, or perhaps where John White did his watercolors. Take part in an event at the gardens, as they have different events and activities throughout the year. Yes, the Elizabethan Gardens are open year round for visitors of any season. So, go enjoy the Christmas lights or the Easter Egg Hunt, or the Elizabethan Luau, or just go. Just walk and enjoy the day.

Oddity ★★

Not strange, perhaps, but certainly impressive to see all those sculptures, statuary, and surprising little unknown bits that, put together, create a really beautiful place to visit.

Difficulty ★★

The Elizabethan Gardens are located in Fort Raleigh National Historic Site, but is run by the Garden Club of North Carolina. There is a fee to enter, but it is well worth the price. Parking usually is no problem, with plenty of marked spots. Take the time to walk through Fort Raleigh and the Lost Colony Theater while you are there.

Statue of Virginia Dare

Manteo 35.93873° -75.71227°

Many people may not look twice at the marble statue of Virginia Dare hidden in the woods of the Elizabethan Gardens. Some may not even notice her as they walk into the sunken gardens, never even looking in her direction. But even if they do, even if they walk right up to her, she could never tell the amazing story of the statue, and how she arrived in the gardens.

The Virginia Dare statue was carved by Maria Louisa Lander, an American artist working in Rome at an art colony there. Lander showed a talent for sculpture early in life, and moved to Rome in her twenties to start a studio there. While in Rome, she met and befriended Nathaniel Hawthorne, a fellow native of her Salem, Massachusetts birthplace. Hawthorne commissioned Lander to carve a bust of him, one of her few works still in existence. While posing for her, Hawthorne became captivated with Lander. She eventually became the model for the free spirited women artists in his novel *The Marble Faun.*

During her time in Rome, she was involved in a scandal that caused her to be shunned by the American art society there. Rumors included stories of an affair and her posing in an improper state of undress for a fellow artist. Even though she received no more commissions, Lander would not let the rumors stop her. She continued to work, carving the Virginia Dare statue out of a column of Carrara marble in 1859. Lander interpreted Dare as she would have looked if she had grown into adulthood, living with the local natives, and dressed as a princess in beads, with only a fishing net wrapped around her waist.

The finished statue was placed on a ship bound for America, but the vessel shipwrecked off the coast of Spain, where the sculpture stayed at the bottom of the sea. The statue was salvaged two years later, and Lander was forced to purchase her own sculpture from the salvagers. It was finally brought to Boston and displayed in an art gallery there. The sculpture was then sold to a collector in New York for the sum of $5000. After the sculpture was delivered to the owner's studio, his building caught fire. If not for a pair of folding doors that had been closed at the time, protecting the statue from the flames, Virginia Dare may have been once again lost, for good. The purchaser of the statue died soon after the fire, and his estate refused to pay for the statue, so Virginia Dare was returned to Lander.

Lander attempted to sell the statue to the Women's Committee of the North Carolina Commission, for display in the 1893 World's Exposition in Chicago, where the state was erecting a building. With no funds available to purchase it, the Women's Committee suggested Lander donate the statue to North Carolina. By this time Lander had moved to Washington, DC, and the statue had become very close to her and she loved it greatly. She decided instead to will the statue to the state. Lander did not die until 1923, and the statue was finally accepted by North Carolina in 1926.

The statue was displayed for some time in the Hall of History in Raleigh. While the statue was exquisite and admirable, some people found the sculpture inappropriate as Virginia Dare was nude, clad only in native beads and a fishing net. Complaints came in that the statue was obscene. It also may have been that the sculpture's placement, beneath the portraits of three Confederate generals, was inappropriate as it seemed the old soldiers were leering at the naked maiden.

When the Hall of History was moved in 1938, Virginia Dare was left behind, placed in the basement of the old Supreme Court Building. For a while she was on display in the office of George Ross Pou, the state auditor, where the naked statue again dredged up some trouble. The sculpture was finally decided to be sent to Waterside Theatre, home of The Lost Colony outdoor drama.

The Lost Colony wanted nothing to do with the statue either. The sculpture was not period correct for the location, and there was no evidence that Virginia Dare had ever grown up with the natives. In fact, most believed she did not survive into adulthood. The statue was then packed away, stored in the same shipping crate she came in, in the backstage area of Waterside Theatre. Albert Q. Bell, the designer of Waterside Theatre, had the statue shipped to the home of Paul Green, the author of The Lost Colony play.

Green kept the sculpture at his home in Chapel Hill, though he never displayed it either, until the Elizabethan Gardens were created by the Roanoke Island Garden Club. He sent the statue to the gardens, where she finally found a home among the woods of her namesake's birthplace.

The sculpture is a lovely, amazing piece, an underappreciated piece of art in a beautiful garden. The story of the statue may overtake the sculpture itself, but the statue is still a work to behold. Some of the little items to notice on the sculpture include the regal heron, perched slightly behind her right leg, and the waves at her feet. The heron may have been a New World representation of the noble hounds placed at the feet of kings in other sculptures. The waves seem to show Virginia as pensive, looking back over the Atlantic Ocean, wondering about her family's native land of England and if one day more ships would come over the horizon to find her.

Oddity ★

The sculpture is nice. The story is pretty amazing.

Difficulty ★★

The Elizabethan Gardens are on the same grounds as the Lost Colony and Fort Raleigh National Historic Site, on the north side of Roanoke Island. You have to pay to get in the gardens, but it's more than worth it. The Elizabethan Gardens are a great place to take an afternoon stroll.

Red Wolf Howl

Highway 64, Dare Mainland 35.86398° -75.86105°

Dare County is generally viewed as a group of islands, a long thin chain of barrier islands covered with sandy scrub brush, and a marshy sound dominated by Roanoke Island. But there is a mainland part of Dare County as well, a giant expanse of empty wilderness, dotted with a few small towns and communities, nestled into woodlands and fields. The vast emptiness is a great place for wildlife to flourish, and the land is abundant with creatures big and small. Turtles dot the creeks, sunning themselves on fallen trees, deer silently amble through the forests, and black bear wander the fields, all content, if not kings, of a fertile and natural land.

Due to the large open land, this area was selected as an outstanding place to reintroduce an animal to the wild, an animal that needed miles and miles to roam, a place to hunt and survive, without threat or interruption.

In the 1960s, the red wolf had gone from being a high end predator that historically roamed throughout the eastern part of the U.S. from Massachusetts down to Florida and as far west as Texas, to a species that was quickly diminishing down to its last few members. Due to massive predator control, where many of the wolves were hunted, as well as extensive habitat loss as more and more land was claimed for human habitation, the red wolf population began to dwindle. In 1967, the red wolf was declared an endangered species, and extensive work was done to find any remaining red wolves in the wild. A small band was discovered in southeast Texas and southwest Louisiana, and some of the animals were collected to be used as a captive breeding program at Point Defiance Zoo in Tacoma, Washington. By 1980, all remaining red wolves had been removed from the wild and placed in breeding programs. At that time, the red wolf was declared extinct in the wild.

Only 17 red wolves were captured from their natural habitat, and of those only 14 were found to be pure red wolves, as 3 shared DNA with coyotes. From those 14, their population slowly grew until the species could be released into the wild. The Alligator River National Wildlife Refuge was chosen as one of the places to attempt the release. Alligator

River was chosen because of the lack of livestock, availability of prey, and lack of coyotes. With livestock operations, the red wolf would pose a problem of hunting the livestock and creating a difficulty with ranch owners, as well as creating a dependence on a human managed food supply, instead of choosing to hunt the more indigenous prey. Coyotes play a risk in that the red wolf will breed with the coyote if there are not suitable mates in their own species, tainting the gene pool.

In 1987, the first release of red wolves occurred at Alligator River, and one year later, the first litter of pups was born. Since then, the red wolf population has grown under the care of the U.S. Fish and Wildlife Service. Today, with an expanded range in eastern North Carolina, the red wolf numbers around 100 in the wild, with a larger number still kept in captive breeding programs across the U.S. Part of the captive breeding program is kept at the Alligator River site, in pens deep in the woods.

While the wolves are there, they are normally not seen by the public, but they can be heard. Wolf Howls are done at the site, starting at Creef Cut Wildlife Trail, just off Highway 64. U.S. Fish and Wildlife offer events in the Spring and Fall, often on a full moon, as well as regular events during the summer on Saturday nights. There is now a fee for the visit, but reservations are not required. Check with the US Fish and Wildlife web site for times and dates.

Attendees meet at the head of the Creef Cut trail parking lot, where they will meet up with their guide. After a short talk, everyone drives down a dusty road to the outskirts of the wolf pens. The wolves are not visible, but soon everyone will know they are there. Usually, the guide will give a call to get the wolves to answer, and then everyone else joins in. Just a word of warning, the wolves can actually get tuckered out after a good howl, and sometimes don't answer on a second try. However, the sound alone is truly as beautiful and haunting as one would think.

So imagine being out in a dusty path, in the middle of the forest, far away from the lights of the islands, tall trees and twinkling stars surrounding you. Then, from the distance, the plaintive wail comes through the trees, and then others, into a baying chorus of some of nature's finest singers. And in this case, you get to sing along.

Oddity ★★★

The red wolf is a naturally shy creature, rarely seen, as it is most active at dusk and dawn. The red wolf has never attacked a human. But they will sing with one.

Difficulty ★★★

This happens only once a week, in the evening, and mostly during the summer. Plus, the drive is a long one from the beaches. Go early, as parking spaces are limited and fill quickly. It is recommended to take insect repellent and a flashlight. Better yet, don't wear any scents to begin with, and leave the light in your pocket to enjoy the wonderful darkness.

Red wolves hunt in small family packs, usually consisting of a mating pair along with pups and juveniles 1 to 2 years old. Older offspring will leave the pack to start their own. Red wolves are very territorial, however, and will vigorously defend their territory. They feed on anything from deer to rabbits, making them excellent natural population control.

Buffalo City

East Lake 35.83735° -75.91907°

We have all seen the sign. Anyone who drives down the lonely road of Highway 64 has noticed it. Riding along, staring out the window at nothing but trees and trees, with the occasional glimpse of a turtle basking in the sun, nothing to break the monotony of the trip. And then you pass it, that sign, innocuous, but also strange. Buffalo City Road. It is the only street sign around. Everyone sees it, everyone wonders, in the back of their mind, "A city? Out here?"

And the answer is yes, out in the middle of nowhere, in the Alligator River National Wildlife Refuge, was a city. More or less.

Buffalo City was a company town built into the mainland part of Dare County back in the 1880s as a logging town for the Eastern Carolina Land and Lumber Manufacturing Company, out of Buffalo, NY. The town was named after the company's home, being given the name Buffalo City Mills. The company brought in a large number of African-American and Russian immigrant laborers to both clear the land and build the town. The town was a simple planned community with identical homes, a school, a post office and general store. Typical of company towns, payment was in a type of scrip called pluck, an aluminum coin that could only be used at the company owned general store.

As soon as the town was functional, logging began. The swampy land was full of prime hardwoods like juniper and cypress, which were well suited for boat boards and shingles, as the wood was impervious to water. The company also harvested the pervasive pine wood that grew readily in the forests. Quickly the business became the largest logging company in northeast North Carolina. The wood could be cut by hand and floated up Milltail Creek to the mill. The wood could then be carried out to Elizabeth City for shipment elsewhere. As logging grew, more modern technology was introduced to Buffalo City and the logging area. Train tracks were laid throughout the land to carry the felled trees to the mills and barges. It is estimated that there were about 100 miles of train tracks laid to help move all the wood from the forest at the height of the company's prosperity.

The town was made up of a large number of workers. At its highest,

Buffalo City was the largest town in all of Dare County at the turn of the 20th century. But even with all the success of the lumber industry, the general populace was all the same kind of poor. The original logging company stayed about 18 years, cutting most of the good lumber, then closing up their mill. In the early 1900s, Dare Lumber Company took over until the 1920s, operating a pulp mill. It later became a family company run by the Duvall brothers. At this time, another form of business became popular in the area, due to a federal law passed in 1920.

Prohibition was the law of the land right at the time when the mill closed down for the last time. In order to make a living, to provide for their families, many residents turned to running stills and bootlegging. Just like with the logs, the people of Buffalo City would ship whiskey out of town on shad boats going up Milltail Creek. Soon, Buffalo City became known for its liquor. The quality of the moonshine was outstanding, as much of the illegal liquor made at Buffalo City was often rye whiskey, which was smoother than corn liquor. The area was ripe for running stills. The water from the creek was clean and tannic, great for distilling. The forest canopy was low and thick, making it difficult for revenuers to find stills hidden in the mainland woods. The only way in at the time was by boat, which made it easy to spot revenuers and other law coming in. Moonshining was definitely a family business, with many people used as lookouts, giving signals to warn of approaching danger. Lots of people got caught, however, and many went to prison for their crimes.

Making moonshine slowed when Prohibition was finally overturned in 1933. Some residents returned to logging, but by then almost all the best

trees had been cut. Disease cut a swath through the town, and later, with jobs and better living available elsewhere, the population dwindled to about 100 people by the 1940s. By 1950, the town was abandoned.

Today, there is little left to see of the old flourishing mill town. There are a few tin roofs still lying on the earth, waiting for groundcover to take over. A couple of falling down buildings still shows up on the gravel road, along with a simple hunting club building. Most of the train tracks are gone, but some rails still exist, and the rail beds are discernible. The town has been given back to the forest from where it came.

Now, Buffalo City is a place for the bears, deer, and alligator. There are roads that lead back into the old area, but mostly the only people that will be back in the woods now will not be moonshiners or revenuers, but kayakers and canoeists. Milltail Creek is now a popular place for paddlers and outdoor adventurers to explore. And who knows? Maybe there's a 5 gallon jug floating around the water somewhere.

Oddity ★★

Okay, nothing much is left. Nothing but a lot of history. So go make it part of your story, it won't take long.

Difficulty ★★

Yes, just turn by the sign and keep driving. But remember, it was not just the loss of the mill jobs that drove the people from Buffalo City. The mosquitoes there don't get many guests, and they get very hungry. The best way to see the area is by water. So if you have a canoe, get out there.

The counter for the general store in Buffalo City was removed before the building fell in, and was used in several restaurants over the years.

Some of the juniper shingles cut at Buffalo City were used on some of the beach houses of the Unpainted Aristocracy, and probably still hang on some today.

Heading to Hatteras

.

Bodie Island Lighthouse

Bodie Island 35.81853° -75.56328°

Bodie Island Lighthouse is an easily accessible light, with a great area for walking and seeing the marsh as well as the wildlife that often visits seasonally. But there is a lot more to the history of the lighthouse, and the island as well. One noticeable thing is that Bodie Island Light is not on an island. And it is not even the original light.

Built in 1872, Bodie Island Light is part of the lighthouse system that stretched across the Carolina coast. It replaced two other lighthouses that bore the same name. The first, built in 1847 and designed by Francis

Gibbons, a skilled lighthouse builder, was unfortunately marred by being overseen by Thomas Blount, who built an unsupported brick foundation for the lighthouse, and the light began leaning seaward within two years. Even after extensive, and expensive, repairs, the light was determined to be unable to be saved. It was abandoned in 1859. This light was built much farther south down the island, where Pea Island is now, and its location is now covered with water.

The second light met a much different fate. At least in a very different way. With a light being needed on the coast, the next Bodie Island Light was built in 1859. The 80 foot tower did not stand long, as the Civil War began with Union military forces quickly taking over the North Carolina coast, including some poorly defended forts around Cape Hatteras and Manteo. Confederate forces, fearing the lighthouse would be used as a spotting tower, packed the base with explosives and blew it to bits.

Congress was reluctant to build a third light at the location, but pressure from ship captains forced the hand of the government to build the third and current light in 1871, using both workers and supplies from the recently completed Cape Hatteras Light. Bodie Island Light was finished in 1872, and the keeper's quarters were added soon after.

While this light was able to stand when its predecessors fell, there were other problems with the light. Being near the water, on a huge migratory highway for geese and other birds, the tower with its first order Fresnel lens would occasionally get struck by migrating fowl. And as the tallest thing for miles and miles, lightning strikes were a problem. Screens and lightning rods helped with those problems, but the isolation of the light was of greater difficulty. During the 1800s, the nearest school in Manteo was accessible only by boat, so it meant that the keeper's family would not be able to live in the quarters except during the summer when school was out. This meant that the keepers would spend most of the year alone on an empty island. It was not until improved roads allowed school buses to be able to get to the lighthouse that the situation changed and the families were able to stay together year round.

The light was altered from the always burning kerosene lamp to a flashing electric light in 1932, and automated in 1940. It currently flashes a light of 2 and a half seconds on, 2 and a half seconds off, 2 and a half seconds on again, and then dark for 22 and a half seconds. Doing so, it flashes this pattern twice a minute.

So the final light went up, and has been shining ever since. It even got a restoration in 2013 which now allows for people to climb the lighthouse for the first time. However, they still need to know how to correctly pronounce the name. Bodie Island is often mispronounced as "bow-dee," but it is actually pronounced like "body." Another confusing part is just how did Bodie Island get its name? Where's the body? And, where's the island?

Well, the Body part is actually very simple. The island was named after a family with the surname Body, or Boddie. On various maps, it can be seen as Body Island as far back as 1729, and Bodies Island in 1775. Curiously, old maps show how many of the islands and place names changed or morphed into new names over the many years. Present day Okracoke is a prime example, with early maps showing its original name to be Wococon. Another illustration of this is in how the island and waters around present day Kill Devil Hills were originally known by the name Colleton, changed to Collinton on its way to Colington. Bodie Island is often rumored to be named for bodies strewn on its shores from ships cracked open during storms, but this is nothing more than legend.

The island part gets a little more confusing. The difficulty is in determining where an island is, or maybe even what an island is. Again, early maps show Bodie Island as a separate landform. In reality, this should not seem surprising. Just look out over the sound to see marsh islands all throughout the area. Bodie Island was once part of a long island chain. While now it is connected to a long thin peninsula running all the way up to the Virginia border, it used to be separate.

How does this happen? Before manmade dunes were put in place on the Outer Banks, there were several areas that were natural weak points on the barrier islands, places where the ocean could easily break through or wash over during storms. Even now these places are easily recognizable. Oregon Inlet is one such spot, as well as the Mirlo Beach area of Rodanthe, where the ocean often overwashes the road during bad storms. New Inlet, near Pea Island, was cut recently by Hurricane Irene in 2011. The breach was so severe that a temporary bridge has been built there as the inlet opens up whenever there is a major storm now.

Long ago, there was a breach north of Cape Hatteras, as well as one in Nags Head, which essentially turned the area in between into an island. Oregon Inlet was not there at the time; it formed in 1846. That island became known first as Body Island, named for its first settlers, and over the years changed to its current spelling of Bodie Island. In that time, the inlets closed and it became part of the larger peninsula.

Now, Bodie Island Lighthouse is an easy drive from the northern beaches. No boats needed, no bridges to cross. Bodie Island Light looks beautiful in any light, and there usually is plenty of parking. The lighthouse is now open for climbing, from late April to Columbus Day in October. There is a fee to tour and climb the lighthouse, and groups are limited to 22 people. Plus, it is not an easy climb, as the lighthouse is cramped, hot, humid, and dusty, as you would expect an old lighthouse to be. But if you want to experience what it was like to be a keeper of the light, you will definitely get that. And if you don't feel like doing all that climbing, enjoy the trails and the view. You may even spend the whole day there just to see the light come on.

Oddity ★

If you do the tour, be sure to look up just inside the base of the lighthouse, above the doorway. There is a sign with the lighthouse name, including its old spelling.

Difficulty ★

Seeing the light is easy, with lots of good views and a big parking lot to find a spot. But the entrance to the lighthouse, from Highway 12, can be easy to miss. The road to the lighthouse is exactly opposite the road that is the entrance to Coquina Beach. Try not to miss it, because the next turn is into the Oregon Inlet marina.

Cape Hatteras Seashore

A Did You See That? Detour

Once people cross over into the Cape Hatteras National Seashore from Nags Head, they can see the obvious change to a place where nature is assertive over the touch of mankind. The land is full of plants and animals, yet so utterly empty of the so common intrusiveness of beach houses and businesses that seem to litter the coast to the north. The first thing a driver would see is essentially nothing. Just scrub brush, marsh grass, sound water, with the occasional flitting bird, rarely a wild fox, often seagulls and pelicans owning the sky. It is a land of beautiful emptiness.

The few spots where humans have intervened stick out in their rarity. Bodie Island Light slowly appears in the sky, while across the street Coquina Beach and its bath house offer a rare access to the sand. Farther down are the Oregon Inlet Fishing Center and the Bonner Bridge, both landmarks, one aging gracefully, one taking a battering. Outside of these places, and few others, the seashore is a place of natural grace. Even farther down into Hatteras, Buxton, Frisco, the old mixes with the new, still villages but with some modern twists.

It may surprise the casual observer that there is a vibrant history in this land, a lot of happenings, a lot of that truly "hidden history" that occurred here. This is just a little bit.

NASA Tracking Dish (or is it?)

When the United States decided to put a man on the moon, the commitment to do so was epic. One of the many things that had to be done was to make sure that mission control in Houston could always stay in contact with the Apollo capsules as they orbited the Earth as well as travelled to and from the moon. Giant tracking dishes were established all across the world, and it was rumored that when NASA discovered a spot in their net that would leave an empty spot in communication, a huge dish was built on Bodie Island.

Here is the curious thing, though. The dish location never appears in any history of NASA's Apollo program. The main dish was large, and accompanied at some time by the smaller communication antenna pictured in this book. The antenna seems to be similar to what was used on Mercury and Gemini programs for communications, but they do not show up in NASA's history either. Were the antennas used for space communications, or was that just a legend to cover up for a more clandestine use? Add to that the giant triangle markers nearby that were supposed to be able to be seen from outer space, and you have a real mystery on your hands.

So, here's the update. It was a tracking dish. But it was not used by NASA. Instead it was used to track missiles starting in the 1960s. Or it may have been a communications relay for secret messages passed along the coast.

The dish sat right on the beach at the southern end of Old Oregon Inlet Road, near where the National Park Service has their storage and supply sheds. The smaller antenna was removed, probably sometime in the 1970s, and the supports were destroyed, cut by torches based on the only other photo of the site. The large dish stood until sometime in the 1980s or 90s, until it was dismantled. It seems no one knows what happened to the giant dish.

It is not there anymore, but it used to be at 35.84625° -75.56416°.

Pea Island National Wildlife Refuge

In 1938, the Pea Island National Wildlife Refuge was established as a place for the nesting and overwintering of migratory birds. The area is part of the Atlantic Flyway, a major thoroughfare of waterfowl on the north-south path of migrating birds.

Today the refuge is home to 365 different bird species, making the area a birder's dreamland. Throughout the year one can see various migrating birds, as well as different shore birds such as pelicans and the endangered piping plover. Peregrine falcons can be spotted fishing in the sound waters. The refuge is over 13 miles long and allows for different accesses for visitors. The sound side land can be accessed through miles of hiking trails that let people easily spy the different birds in the sound or along the shore. Kayakers and canoeists can also get out into the water, and up close to many of the waterfowl that use the sound as a rest stop or for a winter retreat. Swans and geese are regularly seen in the waters. The beach is also part of the refuge, and is a great place for beachcombers to spot shorebirds and fishing birds, such as diving pelicans, as well as many species of gulls.

In addition to the many birders, photographers also love the area. The species of birds change throughout the year, as winter birds move north during the warmer weather, and some tropical birds may appear from time to time. The whole refuge is a wonderful escape, a nice place for a walk in the marshy wilderness where the birds call home and the humans come to visit.

Park and visit at 35.71636° -75.49352°.

Fessenden Radio Broadcast

The beginnings of wireless broadcasting were a rather wild and varied time, with Marconi, Tesla, and others, including Reginald Fessenden, among those who had a hand in early broadcasts of radio. Fessenden did not actually claim to invent radio, but did create several advancements in the development of radio devices and concepts for continuous wave broadcast. Throughout 1901 and 1902, Fessenden set up several towers along the coast to test his ideas. Radio transmission towers sprung up on Roanoke Island, in Hatteras, and south at Cape Henry.

Fessenden's work was supported by the early Weather Bureau as a way to broadcast regional weather forecasts. In 1902, Fessenden was able to send a clear voice broadcast from Cape Hatteras all the way to Roanoke Island. He not only was the first to send a signal over water to ships, but also sent the first musical notes. They were the beginning attempts to show that sound could be carried over the air and understood, that music could be heard and enjoyed. By1906, Fessenden had perfected his work well enough to do public demonstrations of his wireless signals. He became known as the Father of Voice Radio.

There is little left of Fessenden's work on the Outer Banks, at least in the hardware department. His name is still held in high regard, though. Fessenden's name is on the local community center in Hatteras, as well as on a nearby highway marker. The remnants of his Hatteras tower, just the base, are supposedly still visible, but all his towers and stations are now sadly gone. A remnant of tabby, a concrete like substance made of oyster shells, is the only remains of an anchor spot for his tower. It may reside about ten yards away from the southwest corner of the public tennis courts in Buxton, according to legend, but the area is either covered with thick vines and briars, or a skateboard park.

Billy Mitchell Field

Billy Mitchell was an early pioneer of using air power during World War I and the immediate postwar years. Serving as brigadier general of American air power during the war, he utilized lessons learned from Sir Hugh Trenchard, a Royal Air Force commander who advocated the use of separate air power as an offensive weapon, rather than as opportune attacks or reconnaissance only.

After returning to the United States after the Armistice, Mitchell began to espouse the idea of using air power to a greater extent, including the idea of using bomb laden airplanes to destroy the battleships and dreadnoughts that cruised the waters during the past war. He felt that too much money was being spent on building new battleships and other craft, while little was done to build up the more useful airplane fleet that would cost much less than the ships he saw as an easy target for aerial destruction.

His preaching finally reached a head when he arranged to test his idea that an airplane could sink a giant, well armored battleship. In the aftermath of World War I, many ships seized from Germany, as well as obsolete U.S. craft, were to be used as targets for Mitchell's plan. His plan was to drop bombs next to the ships, rather than on them, in order to have the concussion blast in the water rupture the armor plating of the hull, flooding the ships and sinking them.

On September 5, 1923, Mitchell organized an attack on two obsolete battleships, the *New Jersey* and the *Virginia*. He began his attack with his Martin MB-2 bombers leaving from Langley, VA, in order to show the feasibility of a long range attack on ships far out to sea from a land base.

Another group of airplanes left from a temporary field built in Hatteras. The planes attacked the *New Jersey*, leaving her severely damaged, with hull punctures, but still afloat. The attack on the *Virginia* was more direct. Thirteen 1,100 pound bombs were dropped around the ship's hull, caving her in and sinking her in 30 minutes. The planes then rearmed and went out later that day to finish off the *New Jersey*.

Many people did not like Mitchell's outspokenness or his brash disrespect of his superiors, especially when he proved himself right. During a tour of the Pacific in 1924, Mitchell predicted a major victory of air power over naval forces, down to the time and day. He stated that due to Japanese Imperial expansionism, the Japanese naval air fleet will conduct an attack on Pearl Harbor, on a Sunday, commencing at 7:30 am, with a concurrent attack on the Philippines a few hours later. His prescience was uncanny. The Japanese attacked Pearl Harbor on Sunday, December 7, 1941, at 7:55 am, and Clark Field in the Philippines hours later.

Billy Mitchell's insubordination was too much for the military to bear, and he was court-martialed. Instead of accepting the suspension he received, Mitchell left the Army in order to be an outspoken advocate of air power in February of 1926. He unfortunately died of complications of influenza ten years later. Mitchell has been immortalized in many ways since his death, with the recognition of his insight into airplanes as a use of a projection of force. He was honored by Congress with a posthumous Medal of Honor in 1946. Mitchell is also known for changing the look of uniforms for pilots and other airplane personnel. At the beginning of World War I, Army Air Corps personnel were expected to wear the high stiff straight collar of all officers, but it was difficult on their necks as they were constantly scanning the skies for other planes. Most officers

would have lapel collared coats handmade in order to alleviate the itchy collars. Mitchell continued to wear his lapel jackets upon return to the U.S. after the war. By 1926, the uniform was changed for all officers.

And on Hatteras Island, a little player in the huge game of war, where air power had its seeds of greatness sowed, a small airstrip is named after the great aviator who modernized the use of the airplane in warfare. Billy Mitchell field sits at 35.23221° -75.62231°.

Bridge To Nowhere

Near Rodanthe 35.67513° -75.48473°

A bridge is more than an architectural thing. As much as it is a conduit, a link, from one land to another, it can also define the fragility of that connection. Some places are so isolated that the only access is a thin ribbon of road, a narrow path over water built with concrete or wood. Crossing a bridge is often, for the visitor, a sign of entering into the isolation of an island. It is a visible sign of change for the traveler that they have truly entered a different land. Wherever there is water, bridges are important.

In the 1930s on the Outer Banks, a bridge would have been an unnecessary luxury when there were not even roads on the barrier islands. Some people would pay to have their trucks ferried across the sound from Roanoke Island or the mainland. The roads on the Outer Banks were mostly wagon tracks, ruts cut through sand. The best place to drive was actually on the beach, as the smooth, packed sand was a straight path both to wide open beaches down south, and further to the villages along Hatteras Island.

Unfortunately, when a hurricane formed two inlets on Pea Island, the natural beach roads were now blocked by inrushing water. While the inlets were impassible by car, they were too shallow to be forded by ferry. The best solution was to simply build a bridge over each inlet to allow the vehicles to continue their passage. Two wooden bridges were built. As they normally would, the inlets soon closed up and the bridges became unnecessary. After the dunes were created and a paved road was in place to allow easy access all the way down to Hatteras Island, the bridges fell into disrepair.

Today, there are still remnants of the two bridges visible. The northern bridge still has some of its road on the bridge deck and is easily seen from nearby accesses off of Highway 12. All that is left of the southern bridge are its pilings. There is no access to the bridges by wheeled vehicle, but they can be seen up close by boat. Or by pelican.

Oddity ★★

While it may not seem strange to have a bridge over the sound, those old bridges out there, just sitting in the water, home only to the birds, now far away from vehicles, are a little odd, and lonely.

Difficulty ★★★★★

The bridges can be seen easily from the side of the road. Be sure to pull off only at designated parking areas, as the road can be dangerous, and the side of the highway is usually only a good place to get stuck. If you want to see the bridges up close, however, you will need a boat. Pea Island is a great place to go kayaking. The Pea Island Visitor Center offers canoe tours.

Nights in Rodanthe House

Rodanthe 35.60021° -75.46448°

Nicholas Sparks is a prolific writer of intimate romance novels, a novelist who combines an intricate plot with appealing and involved characters, all while existing in a beautiful small town setting. His choice of setting is of particular appeal to his North Carolina readers in that his books usually center on the towns and cities along the east coast of the state. Several of his books have been made into movies, often filmed in the same location as in the book.

His novel, *Nights in Rodanthe*, tells a story of two people, both suffering from loss, separation, and stress in their lives, as they meet at a bed and breakfast in the tiny coastal town. Adrienne Willis tends to the inn that has only one guest, Paul, a doctor looking to escape to the isolation of the quiet barrier islands of the Hatteras seashore. During his stay, a storm blows up, and the two work together to protect the inn from the oncoming tempest. The two fall in love, though after the weekend, they realize they must go back to their other lives. Through letters to each other they slowly heal their wounds, both in their past and current.

The book was made into a movie in 2008, with Diane Lane and Richard Gere playing the two leads.

The movie was popular with fans of Nicholas Sparks' films, as well as appealing to romance movie buffs in general, but for many, the real star was the house. It is a large, multi-story beachfront home, with a high tower attached. Built in the 1980s when the shoreline was hundreds of feet away and in no danger of overwashing the home, it was secured by deep pilings set in concrete. But, as with all things built on the coast, this house could not hold back the sea. By the time of the filming, water lapped at its front pilings. The beach was more beside the house than around it. Storms, surf, and hurricanes took their toll on the building, and soon after filming was completed, the house was condemned. Fans would come to see it, often breaking in to check out the insides, not knowing the interior did not match the film. The water and septic lines had all been washed away, and the house was not livable. The ocean would regularly send waves under the house, turning it into an improbable and incongruous island.

The owners had little choice but to let the house sit, and hope against hope that something would happen to save the house.

Then, with the house nearly at its end, Ben Huss, of Newton, NC, purchased the house in order to preserve and restore it. And happily, he delivered on his plans. Ben and his wife Debbie bought the house in January of 2010. Within days the house was removed from its pilings, jacked up onto a truck and hauled down the road to a new piece of property farther back from the ocean with more dune protection. Once relocated, the house was restored inside and out. For the film, the building had been outfitted with decks and blue shutters, but they were removed when filming ended. These were recreated and added to the house at its new location. Interior shots were actually done on a soundstage, so the inside of this beach house looked nothing like the one in the movie. Because of this, the new owners went to great lengths to recreate the inside of the house, redoing the kitchen and adding special touches seen in the film. Swinging doors, unique blue wallpaper, an antique bed with tall headboard, and even a pump organ were all located to be placed in the house.

Now the house is finished, saved and preserved. It has since been named Serendipity, and is up for rent for fans of the movie, as well as anyone else who just wants a really nice place to stay on the peaceful Rodanthe beach. The house never actually was a bed and breakfast, and is now rented out for the whole house. With 6 bedrooms, a hot tub, and great beach access, Serendipity now lends itself more to a fun vacation for a family now, rather than a weekend stay for two during a storm. Which, considering how the story ends, may be more fitting.

Oddity

Serendipity now stands as a very nice beach house in Mirlo Beach, but it used to stand as a monument both to mankind's attempt to hold back the seas, as well as the relentlessness of the ocean. So enjoy the hot tub!

Difficulty ★

The house is technically a private residence. It is not open for tours, and usually is rented in the summer, so don't go thinking you can walk in to see the insides, unless you rent it. Serendipity stands on private property on a short access road, so driving by to get a picture is probably okay.

Many of the interior shots were done on a soundstage in Wilmington, but some interiors were shot at a house on Topsail Island.

San Delfino British Cemetery

Buxton 35.24810° -75.53328°

At the beginning of World War II, the U.S. found itself unprepared for a war in the Atlantic. After the surprise attack on Pearl Harbor, the U.S. Navy had committed many of its ships to the island hopping pursuit of the Japanese fleet in the Pacific. At the same time, Nazi Germany had declared war upon the U.S. as part of its pact with Japan. This brought about a ruinous and demoralizing secret plan, formed by Rear Admiral Karl Donitz, a U-boat commander. Operation *Paukenschlag*, or Drumbeat, was put into place in Mid December of 1941. Up until that time, the U-boats had not been allowed to target any American ships heading to Europe with war supplies, as they were not at a state of war with the U.S. But this time, the gloves were off for the Germans.

On January 13, 1942, 5 U-boats were in place off the eastern seaboard, and all struck targets on that day. By February 6, the U-boats had sunk 25 ships before heading home. The mission had proved so successful that more U-boats were sent to the Atlantic coast. Operation Drumbeat was really only the first of many submarine attacks. The torpedoes kept coming for the merchant ships along the Atlantic seaboard.

Soon, the U-boats came in waves, and the commanders had begun to use a refueling submarine, called a milkcow, to further extend their range. The U-boat commanders especially favored the waters of Cape Hatteras. The promontory was a navigational landmark that many ships' captains used. The area became so embattled that cargo ship captains gave the place the nickname "Torpedo Junction." The U.S., even though warned by the British of this oncoming danger, was woefully unprepared. Not only were there few patrol craft available, or used, other strategies such as blackout restrictions on shore were not in place at the time. While the U-boats patrolled at night, they could watch the well lit coastline, and when a ship would pass between them and land, it would be silhouetted against the nighttime lights of towns, villages, or even car headlights. It did not help that early on, the ships themselves would sail with their running lights lit. For the experienced German commanders, it was easier than target practice. For months the attacks came, and the ships went down in flames. Legend tells that the ships would burn so intensely at night that one could read a newspaper from the light of the inferno off shore. The cargo ships carrying supplies to the war effort on the other side of the Atlantic paid a price for unpreparedness, and the butcher's bill was steep.

It took about 6 months for the U.S. Navy to finally realize the danger of this effort to cripple the supply chain to the war front. By summer, the lights were off, both in towns and even on the tall Cape Hatteras Lighthouse. Ships now cruised in convoys, and patrol ships, formerly offered by the British and now finally accepted, prowled the water while air patrols, including blimps from nearby Weeksville LTA naval base, scoured the ocean from the skies, looking for the telltale shapes of Nazi U-boats in American waters. By May, ships were sailing in zigzagging convoys, and sinkings were going down in number. U- boats became hunted, with 7 submarines meeting their final end on the east coast. Only 40 sailors were rescued from the subs, with 302 Germans lost. In contrast, over the 6 months of hunting, the German U-boats sank 397 ships, killing approximately 5000 sailors and sending about 2 million tons of ships and supplies to the Atlantic's deep.

One of those 397 ships was the *San Delfino MV*. A tanker for Eagle Oil and Shipping, the *San Delfino* was on its way from Houston to Halifax, Nova Scotia, and on toward Great Britain carrying 11,000 tons of aviation fuel. Crossing Torpedo Junction on April 9, 1942, the *San Delfino* was torpedoed by the German U-boat U-203, commanded by Kapitänleutnant (Lieutenant Commander) Rolf Mützelburg. Of the 42 crew members on the *San Delfino*, 28 were lost.

The body of one sailor was recovered from the *San Delfino* after washing ashore nearly a month after the attack. Fourth Engineer Officer Michael Cairns, of the Royal Merchant Navy, was laid to rest in a small cemetery on Hatteras Island, near Cape Hatteras Lighthouse. Nearly a year later, the HMS *Bedfordshire* was torpedoed near Ocracoke, and while most of the bodies were recovered there, one unknown sailor washed ashore in Hatteras and was interred with Cairns.

The gravesite is still well kept by the National Park Service. It is found on NPS land at Cape Hatteras Lighthouse. At the head of the Open Ponds Trail is a small plot of land with the two grave markers, surrounded by a low white fence. The land, like the more famous British cemetery located in Ocracoke, is leased to the British government and is considered British soil.

Oddity ★★

The graveyard is more delicate and modest than the Ocracoke cemetery. Older gravesites are somewhat common in the backwoods of the Outer Banks, but they usually are still on American soil.

Difficulty ★★

The British Cemetery at Cape Hatteras is located at the beginning of the Open Ponds Trail, just off of the parking lot. The trail head is located a little ways past the turnoff for the lighthouse, and past the picnic area, on Lighthouse Road. Parking is limited to about three cars at a time. Note the name of the trail, Open Ponds. If you decide to hike it, you will find several ponds along the trail, which only add to the number of flying pests one may encounter on this walk. Take some repellent, and wear good shoes.

Kapitänleutnant Rolf Mützelburg met a rathr gruesome and ingloriou end to his life. He died during World War II, but rather than perishing in battle, he died from a freak accident. Taking a break to enjoy a swim in the water of the Azores, he dove from the conning tower just as the deck lifted from a freak swell. Mützelburg struck the deck with his head and shoulder. He died before a doctor could arrive from another U-boat. He was buried at sea.

Young readers, and adults, too, will enjoy Nell Wise Wechter"s book, *Taffy of Torpedo Junction*, a tale of a young Hatteras Island girl who experiences the beginning of World War II from the bedroom window of her grandfather's fishing shack on the beach

So many tankers were sunk along the Outer Banks that the oil and tar balls washed up for decades. Locals knew to keep paper towels and bottles of corn oil on hand at their beach houses to wipe the oil stained heels of anyone who had been strolling on the beach. Spots of tar could be found on the beach after storms even in the 1980s.

Cold War Submarine Detection Cables

Buxton 35.25631° -75.51959° (cables are not always visible)

After World War II, with the relative success of submarine warfare now firmly entrenched as part of necessary weaponry for any powerful nation, the submarine became a major threat to any seagoing military. The U.S. and its now NATO partners along the Atlantic Ocean had seen the damage that a pack of submarines could do to shipping, as well as to naval warships. Technology had made major jumps during the war, and new detection technology was continually being pressed into service.

One of the new pieces of equipment being used was called SOSUS, an acronym for Sound Surveillance System. Conceived in 1949, SOSUS was meant to be a listening system for the threat of Soviet submarines. The USSR had a large fleet of diesel subs at the time. The basic idea was to place listening posts along the ocean to hear the low frequency sound of the submarines as they crossed the Atlantic from the cold weather ports of Russia all the way down toward the Caribbean. After testing the system, in 1952 the cables were laid in the ocean under the name of Operation Caesar. While this was happening, the Navy began building listening posts on the coasts where the cables would come to shore. These small bases were given the colorful name of NAVFAC, which simply was a shortened form of Naval Facility, a more colorless term to hide any interest in what was actually happening inside that naval facility.

The cables were strung in a loop across the Atlantic, but since they could only be extended 150 miles each, the NAVFACs needed to be located on a spot where the continental shelf edge was close to shore. One of those spots happened to be Cape Hatteras. A facility was opened there on January 11, 1956. Hatteras Island of the day may have been somewhat isolated, but it probably was not a bad place to be assigned. The sailors probably enjoyed the beach and sound when not listening for Soviet submarines.

Once the cables were laid, SOSUS went active in 1961. Its first test was to track the USS *George Washington*, a nuclear powered ballistic missile submarine, as it crossed the Atlantic from Connecticut to Scotland. Proving itself successful, SOSUS began listening for the Soviets.

It did not have to listen long. In June of 1962, the NAVFAC base in Cape Hatteras made contact with a Soviet diesel submarine. It was the first contact that SOSUS was able to pick up of an enemy sub. A month later, a Soviet nuclear sub was detected by the NAVFAC in Barbados.

SOSUS functioned exceptionally for years. It was able to track and place virtually all of the rather noisy Soviet submarines easily, up through the 1970s. Tracking became more difficult because of the 1985 revelation that John Walker, a U.S. Navy officer, had revealed information about SOSUS to the Soviets during his 17 years as a spy for the Soviet Union. Once the USSR had learned of the listening system, they went on a crash course of creating more soundproof submarines, less detectible to the underwater hydrophones of SOSUS.

The listening system was upgraded throughout the years, becoming more automated, with less need for numerous bases. It was also augmented with other listening systems, such as towed arrays on ships at sea. But ultimately, SOSUS could not survive the end of the Cold War. With fewer and fewer threats of large nuclear powered submarines in the Atlantic, much of SOSUS was replaced with simpler devices that could detect submarines nearby them. On June 30, 1982, the SOSUS naval facility at Hatteras was deactivated, and more followed. Now only three NAVFACs still are operational to receive the data. But the cables remain in the ocean.

And maybe onshore. The SOSUS cables had to come ashore to get their information to the facilities that processed it. While the base is no longer on Hatteras Island, the cables could still be seen running into the water for many years, when the beach sand was eroded. The base was completely removed in recent times, but the cables may not have been pulled up. They may be uncovered after a good storm. Go have a listen.

Oddity★★★

A big old electrical cable running out into the water just seems like a bad idea. Did anyone unplug this thing first?

Difficulty★★★

Remember that the cables were originally hidden for a reason, and they may not be visible when you visit. On busy days, the parking lots can get crowded, and it might be a bit of a walk, but that is about the only problem you may have. Unless you are a Russian submarine.

The Cape Hatteras Lighthouse was in danger of falling into the ocean as it sat close to the water's edge. In 1999, it was moved 2,900 feet from its original location to a place southwest, about 1600 feet from the shore, The foundation stones were left in place, with the names of all the lighthouse keepers and assistant keepers carved into them. The stones have been moved inland from the original site to make a small outdoor amphitheater.

SOSUS is still used to detect migratory patterns of whales and the use of illegal drift netting.

Cora Tree

Frisco 35.26128° -75.59113°

The twisted oaks that cover much of Hatteras Island are a pretty common sight throughout the many communities there, but no other tree has a story quite like the Cora Tree, which sits in the middle of the road in a housing development in Frisco.

The Cora Tree has a legend tied to it, the type of legend that that is often told throughout the Outer Banks, but this one has a twist. More about that at the end, just so the surprise is not ruined.

Sometime in the 1700s, in one of the quiet fishing villages that dotted the Hatteras coast, there was a strange, mysterious woman named Cora that lived in an old shack in the soundside forest. She lived only with a small child, a "knee baby," as is often called in the legend. Both woman and child were peculiar. Cora and her child lived alone, with no man ever appearing at the house. The child did not act like a typical toddler, but always stared at others with a peculiar frown. But the people of Hatteras were at least tolerant of peculiarities, if not accepting of her strangeness. They paid her little mind, and gave her a wide berth, leaving her be for the most part.

Strange things occurred on the occasions she appeared, though. The local fishermen knew the vagaries of their profession. Days may be good or bad, and no matter their skill, there may be a trip out to sea where their nets would come back empty. But Cora always seemed to have plenty of fish. Once, when walking by a cow, she brushed up against it, and the cow went dry, never to give milk again. And most peculiar was when a boy of the village taunted Cora's baby, only to come down with a fever that night and almost die. Many suspected her of being a witch, but rather than cause more problems, the local islanders just gave her some extra space.

Had Cora lived in the north of the country at the time, like in Salem, Massachusetts, she would not have had an easy time of it, but living in the more tolerant southern coast, it took an act by a displaced and displeased visitor to bring things to a head. Shipwrecks were a common occurrence, and brought the human flotsam along with any broken ship with it. In this way, Captain Eli Blood and his band of freed slaves from

Barbados found their way to the coast of Hatteras. After his ship foundered on the shoals and broke apart, the captain and crew were made guests of the island until help could come from up north to save what was left of the ship's cargo, as well as rescue the crew. Captain Blood made his home as a guest of one of the many fishing boat captains while his crew happily pitched camp under the ships' sails on the beach. The balmy days and beautiful beach made for relatively easy, if boring, living for the seafarers. Captain Blood in due course learned the story of Cora the witch, but aside from some Puritanical grumbling, it does not seem like he did anything about it. That is, until a young man, an upstanding and highly regarded member of the village, was found dead on the beach one morning. Flat on his back in the wet sand, his hands were clasped together at his chest, and the number 666 was burned into his forehead. His face was a rictus of terror. There was no evidence of the cause of death, but a set of footprints led away from the body, into the woods. The tiny prints were the match of a light woman, and quickly, suspicion turned to Cora.

Captain Blood rounded up his crew and went to Cora's shack to capture and question her, as only a Salem preacher would. Cora was bound, hand and foot, and prepared for her first test. Knowing that a witch would use her magic to save herself from drowning, Blood and crew threw her into the calm shallows of the sound, only to find that she floated. Captain Blood, a self proclaimed witch hunter, felt that proved her to be a witch, for if she was human she surely would have sunk and drowned. Blood took no mind that the sound water was not deep enough for just about anyone to drown. He then pulled Cora from the sound, and proceeded to his second step. Drawing his knife, he attempted to cut her hair. His blade found it impossible, and he declared her hair to be like wire. Finally, in an attempt to divine truth from the spirit world, Blood and his crew all cut their fingers to drip blood into a vessel of water, stirring it until it foamed. Peering into the murky sanguine mess, they all stated they saw Cora, conversing with the Devil himself.

Thus proven, at least to their satisfaction, Blood took action. The townsfolk were aghast, but dreaded interference in the profane actions for fear of the wrath of either Blood or Cora. Captain Blood and his crew tied Cora and her child together, bound to a large live oak tree. Then they gathered kindling to place at her feet. One of the townspeople cried out for him to spare the child, but to no avail. Blood was set to his task. At the last moment, as Blood approached with a lit torch, one man tried to stay his hand. Captain Tom Smith pleaded with Blood, stating that whether or not she was a witch, she should be tried in the courts for the murder, not killed this way. As he said that, he heard gasps from the crowd. Cora's child began to hiss and spit, and the babe transformed in front of their eyes into a ferocious wild cat. With this act, all intervention by the townsfolk stopped.

But another intervention was occurring at the same time. Clear skies became inky black, as a thunderstorm roiled in the atmosphere. All the spectators, sailors and local alike, looked on in wonder. Captain Blood, his spine stiffened, approached Cora and her feline to light them afire. Before he could approach, a giant bolt of lightning crackled out of the sky, striking a cacophonous blow to the tree.

The entire group was knocked down, stunned by the shock. When they finally recovered, shaky from the experience, they all noticed the smell of sulfur in the air. The tree had been struck, and was split down the middle, smoking from the bolt. But, mysteriously, Cora and her cat had disappeared. The ropes were still tied tight around the trunk of the tree, but Cora and the wild feline were gone. The tree was burned down the middle, smoking and split.

The story ends at that point, except for one little item. The tale seems odd, just a legend, right? It hardly can be true that this occurrence actually happened, except for one thing. While there was no trace of Cora or her cat, there was one mark left after her disappearance; the name CORA was carved into the tree, burned into the trunk, as if by a fiery pointed finger, a reminder of who had been there and what had happened. To this day, the letters can still be seen in the tree.

Oddity ★★★★

The tale is pretty weird just in general. What's really strange is that the letters have stayed in the tree, never grown over. What's even stranger? Cora's wild cat, a strange furry beast with piercing green eyes and a deep red mouth, so unlike the usual witch's black lap kitty, has been seen over the years in many parts of North Carolina.

Difficulty ★★

The tree is on Snug Harbor Drive in Brigands Bay down in Frisco. With the story so legendary, but with the twist of the letters carved in the bark, many people go by to see it. You will have to go to the tree to see the letters, but maybe don't touch it...

The Captain Blood of this story is referred to as Captain Eli Blood by Charles Harry Whedbee in his book *Blackbeard's Cup and Stories of the Outer Banks*, the book that made the story famous. Captain Blood does not seem to have a relation to the novel character Captain Blood or and pirate captains, and seems to be a respectable, if overzealous, ship's captain. While he is made out to be vicious, it should be pinted out that Captain Blood did turn out to be right, and Cora actually was a pretty evil witch in the legend.

UFO House

Frisco 35.24865° -75.60875°

Aliens haven't landed in Frisco. Well, if they did, they left their UFO behind a long time ago.

The UFO perched in Frisco is actually a unique building called a Futuro home. In 1968, Matti Suuronen, a Finnish architect, designed the Futuro home as a prefabricated metal and plastic design meant to be assembled in pieces on its final land site. The Futuro was a round dome prebuilt in sections in a factory. They were either shipped to the homeowner's land and assembled there, or put together at one location and flown in completed to their final plot by helicopter. The building is designed to stand on four legs, so all the Futuro needed to be constructed was four concrete pads upon which to rest. It was meant to be the house of the future, but with rising plastic prices, the Futuro never made the impact it was meant to make. There were only about 100 Futuros ever built worldwide, and fewer than 60 are known to still exist. Frisco is the current location of one of the few Futuro homes still around.

The UFO house originally sat on the west side of Highway 12, and has operated as a hot dog stand and a retail store for a while, with a day-glo green paint scheme. The Frisco UFO was repainted in shiny silver sometime in the year 2000.

It was moved to the east side of the road by the current owner. Even that has a rather curious story to it. While the Futuro was meant to be easily moved by helicopter or truck, in this case it was Hatteras islander ingenuity that got the thing moved over. Owner Leroy Reynolds got some help and lifted it onto a large flatbed truck early one morning so there would be little traffic as it moved down the road. He sat on top with a pole to move the telephone wires and got it onto its current plot of land before anyone noticed.

The UFO house sat unrepaired for a while, but due to its growing popularity, it has been fixed up. The paint has been cleaned up, the interior cleaned and opened, and the outside decorated with various colorful alien artifacts. And if visitors are lucky, the alien pilot, owner Reynolds in a race suit and mask, may even show up.

Oddity ★★★

This UFO house is pure weirdness and is extremely rare.

Difficulty ★

The UFO house sits right off of Highway 12 on the ocean side of the road in between Buxton and Frisco. You won't have to get out of the car, unless they use the tractor beam on you.

Look at the windows to find the little alien enjoying a scoop of ice cream. It's a remnant from the Futuro's snack bar days.

Graveyard of the Atlantic Museum

Hatteras 35.20627° -75.70409°

The story of the Graveyard of the Atlantic Museum is an old one, much older than most would know. It actually starts on the evening of December 30, 1862, as Commander Stephen Trenchard helms his ship, the USS *Rhode Island*, across the treacherous shoals of Cape Hatteras, towing precious cargo toward the Union blockade of Wilmington. As the weather deteriorates, the ship he tows, a top heavy flat bottomed boat that is better suited for river passage than the open ocean, begins to flounder. Its crew signals they are in danger, but there is no saving the craft as it bucks in the high seas.

Before the morning will come, four officers and twelve enlisted sailors will have died, and the USS *Monitor* will have sunk to the sandy ocean floor of the Graveyard of the Atlantic.

Move forward to August of 1973, as researchers from Duke University test using geological survey equipment for finding underwater archeological sites and shipwrecks. They discover several ships in their search, but only one has the distinctive shape of the *Monitor*. After over 110 years, the USS *Monitor* had been found.

It had always been known that the *Monitor* had sunk off the coast of Hatteras somewhere, but now there really was a treasure out there. And based on the photos, the ship was still fairly well put together, even though it had capsized and the turret was underneath the stern of the ship. Some damage had occurred during the sinking, and the wreckage probably had been damaged by depth charges during World War II, but the ship was pretty much there. With artifact recoveries beginning, Hatteras Village was encouraged to ask for items from the wreck, including the coveted turret. Since there existed no museum on Hatteras Island at the time, the next step was to build one. Over many years, funds and plans were made for the museum, and finally the museum broke ground in December of 1999. The 18,000 square foot building was designed to withstand a 1000 year flood and hurricane force winds, but unfortunately it did not have the resources to do complex restorations needed on many of the *Monitor* artifacts. The Mariners' Museum in Newport News, Virginia received the engines, propeller, anchor, and the coveted turret with cannons in 2007.

So the Graveyard of the Atlantic Museum did not receive the turret of the *Monitor*. It did get many other artifacts, including the Enigma coding machine recovered from the German submarine *U-85*, sunk in April of 1942 by the USS *Roper*. It was the first submarine sunk by the American Navy during the war. The Enigma machine was of supreme importance for the Germans, as well as the Allies. The Germans were convinced throughout the war that the Enigma signals were not decodable, while the British had actually cracked the Enigma and could decode messages in a day or two. The museum's Enigma machine has been undergoing conservation with parts already in the museum and the rest will be on display once finished.

While the Graveyard of the Atlantic Museum did not get the turret to the *Monitor*, it may have been a blessing in the end. The turret is at the Mariner's Museum in Virginia, where it was placed in a giant vat of sodium hydroxide and water to promote desalinization of the wrought iron. The process will probably take over twenty years to complete.

Fortunately, there are many more objects on display, on loan from various collections, but there are two items that deserve special attention. One is big, gigantic, impossible to miss, since it is a giant Fresnel lens from the Cape Hatteras Lighthouse. The other one is innocuous, a little item that is part of the museum that most people would look at once, and then move on. Which is too bad, because it is a small part of a huge ship, and a huge story. Behind glass sits the windlass from the sailing ship *Caroll A. Deering*.

Caroll A. Deering Windlass

The *Caroll A. Deering* is a legend among shipwrecks, a truly amazing story of a ghost ship that found its way to the Cape Hatteras coast. On January 29, 1921, the five-masted schooner was sailing back from Rio de Janeiro via Barbados to Hampton Roads, Virginia, when it was spotted by the Cape Lookout Lightship. The lightship keeper noted that a redheaded sailor reported that they had lost their anchors. The next evening, the *Deering* was spotted by the SS *Lake Elon*. By January 31, the *Deering* had run aground on the shoals of Cape Hatteras. The morning light showed her to the Coast Guard station on Cape Hatteras as wedged firmly on the sandbar, its decks awash. Due to the rough seas, no one could get to the ship until February 4, when the ship *Rescue* and the cutter *Manning* arrived on site. Captain James Carlson, skipper of the *Rescue*, boarded the *Deering* and found a very strange sight.

The ship, though stranded, did not appear wrecked. Its sails were furled, and food in the galley was laid out for the next meal. All personal effects were gone, as well as key navigational equipment, charts, and maps. The ship's log was also missing. Two of the *Deering*'s lifeboats were also absent from the deck. Every sign of the crew seemed to have disappeared. The only living thing still on the ship was a cat.

Attempts to salvage the ship were made, but proved impossible. With it breaking apart on the shoals, it was towed away and dynamited.

Soon, an investigation was started into the disappearance of the crew. Various theories abounded at the time. Was the crew lost during a hurricane? Did they have to abandon ship in a storm? Was it pirates who boarded the *Deering*, making the crew and captain walk the plank like days of yore? Was the ship a target of rum runners, looking for a fast boat to carry their illicit liquor? Even Communist pirates were suspected, with the threat of them stealing ships and taking them to Russia. Even more far out theories circulated, as the *Deering* had passed through the infamous Bermuda Triangle. Perhaps aliens snatched the crew into some early 1900s flying saucer? Or was it something much simpler, like mutiny?

The strange mystery may have a rather straightforward explanation when other facts are considered. The *Deering* left for Rio with its captain, William H. Merritt, and Merritt's son, Sewell, who served as first mate. Captain Merritt crewed a ship of ten sailors. Two days into the voyage, Captain Merritt became ill and had to put in to port. He and his son went ashore, while the crew recruited a retired captain, W.B. Wormell, to continue the voyage. Charles McLellan was also hired as first mate. The ship continued to its destination of Rio, where Captain Wormell met with another skipper, and discussed his distrust of the crew. First Mate McLellan was equally unimpressed with his captain. After too much drunken revelry in Barbados, McLellan was heard threatening to kill Captain Wormell before they landed at Hampton Roads, their final destination. McLellan was thrown in jail, but Wormell for some reason forgave him for the comments and bailed him out before setting sail on January 9.

In between that time and the stranding of the *Deering*, something happened to the captain, as well as the crew. The redheaded

sailor seen by the Diamond Shoals Lightship was definitely not Captain Wormell, and probably not even an officer. Other sailors were seen milling about the deck, which was highly suspicious of a large sailing vessel like the Deering. No one knows what happened in that time, as the captain, first mate, and crew all vanished. While mutiny was the most likely cause of the abandonment of the *Deering*, there still seemed to be many unanswered questions. If the crew killed Captain Wormell, why did they abandon the ship instead of sailing it to another country? Were all of the crew in on the mutiny, and if so, where did they end up? If the crew left the ship in the lifeboats, they should have put to shore somewhere nearby. They couldn't have gone far in tiny boats. Investigators searched other ships for the missing crew in order to question them, but none were found. Ultimately, the general consensus was that the crew had mutinied, but had then been lost to the ocean in a storm or hurricane. The investigation ended in 1922 with no conclusion. Even though that was the end of the *Deering*'s story, that actually was not the end of the *Deering*. Locals had always been resourceful in using whatever drifted upon their shores, including ship's pieces. The ship's keel wound up on the shore, which made it easier to pilfer the lumber. Some of the *Deering*'s wood ended up as supports to locals' homes. Soon the remains of the ship had disappeared from view. But one piece does survive. The windlass of the *Deering* sat for years in front of Wheeler Balance's Texaco station in Hatteras Village, a memento of the great mystery. It was a popular photo opportunity on families' journeys along Highway 12. The windlass now is visible at the Graveyard of the Atlantic Museum, the only artifact left from the famous ghost ship.

Oddity

Seeing a rusty windlass is not much of a trophy, but the story behind it is unique. Most ghost ship tales rest solely in legend. This happened in the 20th century, and has never been fully solved.

Difficulty ★★

The windlass has been behind glass during restoration, but may be out on display. The only extra difficulty in seeing this is that a donation is expected to see much of the items within the museum's main exhibit area.The complete collection, and the cause, are well worth it.

Locals were known to take advantage of whatever they could recover from shipwrecks fro their own use. Some would even use the flags and pennants from ships as blankets by sewing them into quilts or adding wool to them.

The story of the *Carroll A. Deering* was turned into a haunted ghost ship in Nags Head in the 1980s. Built almost to scale, the giant "ghost ship" was opened as a walk through haunted house style tour.The giant wooden ship stood in Nags Head until it burned to the ground years later.

On April 11, 1921, Christopher Columbus Gray of Buxton produced a message in a bottle that stated "DEERING CAPTURED BY OIL BURNING BOAT SOMETHING LIKE CHASER. TAKING OFF EVERYTHING HANDCUFFING CREW. CREW HIDING ALL OVER SHIP NO CHANCE TO MAKE ESCAPE. FINDER PLEASE NOTIFY HEADQUARTERS DEERING." It was later determined to be a forgery.

Original Cape Hatteras Lighthouse Lens

Another major display, and easily noticed, is the original Cape Hatteras Lighthouse first order Fresnel lens. The lens has a rather convoluted history, which follows the path of destruction that happened to eastern North Carolina during the early days of the Civil War. But that was only the beginning. Or, maybe, that was the middle of the story.

The beginning of the tale probably goes all the way back to a burgeoning new United States, hopeful in its growth of trade. Ships coming up from the Caribbean toward large port cities in the north must pass the treacherous Graveyard of the Atlantic, an often stormy and perilous area where the Gulf Stream and Labrador currents churn the water while hidden sandbars and shoals reach up to grab unsuspecting ships. Realizing that something had to be done to protect the sailing vessels passing by daily, as well as nightly, the fledgling government built a lighthouse on the promontory of Cape Hatteras and lit it in 1803. The original light was only 90 feet tall, and built on a low hill to help with the elevation of the light. While the beam could be seen about 12 to 18 miles to sea, depending on weather, its light was feeble and often not lit, with a rather pathetic oil lamp and reflector source for the light. A keeper had to be continually available to clean the reflectors and make sure the light would be relit. Ships found the light so unreliable that they almost preferred to have no light, as the intermittent appearance could confuse mariners. Were they seeing Cape Hatteras or the lights from a steamer? Was the light out, or were they still too far from the beach to see it? The complaints and dangers were so numerous that something had to be done.

The lighthouse was continually refurbished in an attempt to make it functional. The tower was raised to 150 feet, and a new lantern room was built on top. This was done to accommodate the prize of the U.S. Lighthouse Board, a first-order Fresnel lens, which was installed in the lighthouse in 1854. The Cape Hatteras Lighthouse, now a mixture of granite and sandstone, was painted red and white in an effort to mask its drab appearance.

The prize lamp would not shine for long. The outbreak of the Civil War had North Carolina woefully ill prepared for naval warfare at its shores, but one thing the state could do was to turn off the beacons of the coastal lighthouses that would normally aid Union ships as they passed the Carolina coast. So the light was ordered to be put out by the governor of North Carolina, the Honorable John W. Ellis. The lens was disassembled by a chagrined and somewhat reluctant lighthouse keeper, Benjamin Fulcher, and hidden from Union forces in the event of an invasion. Thus began an amazing tale of the travels of the lens of Cape Hatteras.

Carefully packed up into crates, the numerous lenses, as well as the frame for the light, began a trip from the coast that would keep them hidden from Union forces tasked with reacquiring the light throughout the war, and ultimately, in a way, keep the light hidden for 150 years afterwards.

The lens would travel by wagon, by boat, by rickety Confederate train, from the coast inland, narrowly missing being recaptured by Union soldiers, whose superiors were desperate to regain the light. First stored in Washington, the lens' location would probably have been gleaned by spies for General Burnside. The Hatteras lens had taken on a value greater than its actual worth, a prize both to be won by the Union army, and denied by those entrusted with its safekeeping from an advancing occupying force. It moved out of Washington just ahead of advancing Union gunboats on the last ship out of the wharf, heading further inland to Tarboro. From there the lens was repacked carefully for an arduous trip by rail, a unique event as most trains were being used to transport large artillery pieces at the time, to Granville County. It made the journey to a small town in Granville County, where its chaperone, Dr. David Tayloe, reported that he had placed the entire light contents into "a good store house in the county and safely stored." It was a good hiding place, indeed.

Since the original lens was missing from the Cape Hatteras tower, a new first order Fresnel lens was acquired and put in its place, relighting the dangerous passage. But the other lights of North Carolina at Cape Lookout, Bodie Island, and the many lenses from the sounds of North Carolina were unlit and missing as well.

The end of the war saw Union General Sherman marching with his troops toward Raleigh, unprotected after Confederate General Johnston's attempt to slow their march with an attack on Sherman's flank at Bentonville. The worry was that Raleigh would meet the same fate as other cities did at the business end of Sherman's torch. Fortune smiled on Raleigh, as Lee surrendered his troops, essentially ending the war, while Sherman was on still on Raleigh's outskirts. Instead of burning Raleigh, Sherman was able to occupy it. Upon entering the capital building, devoid of southern representatives, Union troops discovered that stored safely there were crates and crates of valuable lighthouse parts, lenses and framework, all from the empty lighthouses along the coast. Included was one first-order lens. But after inspection, it was found to be the lens from Cape Lookout. The prize lens from Hatteras was still missing.

It was not until six months after the war ended that the lens was found, relatively safe, in that good store house in little Townsville, near the Virginia border. Tucked away in crates, the lens had finally been found. Its pedigree determined, the Cape Hatteras Light was then sent to Staten Island, New York, the home for the Lighthouse Board and its lights.

In desperate need of lenses, the Lighthouse Board made the decision to send the many lights it had back to France for refurbishing, rather than spend the money on new lenses. The Cape Hatteras light was sent over to the Henry-LePaute lens factory in France to have lenses replaced and polished. At the same time, the old Cape Hatteras lighthouse was in such disrepair, and close to falling over, that a new tower was being built in its place. This is where the confusion would set in for many, and how the original lens "disappeared." Originally, the intention was to build the new tower, which is the current lighthouse, and then move the lens of the old lighthouse over to the new tower. The issue was that to carefully disassemble the lens, lower it down one lighthouse, then raise the fragile glass and reassemble the light at the top of the new tower would take several days. Days that would leave the coast without a light. The Lighthouse board offered a solution. Place a "new" light atop the new lighthouse. That way, the new Cape Hatteras Lighthouse could be turned on the night after the old light would be extinguished. The only issue was that what the Lighthouse Board meant as "new" was really the old Cape Hatteras lens, the original that was taken almost a decade ago. What they really meant was different, meaning refurbished, not brand new.

To further confuse the issue was that the country was building lighthouses all over, wherever there was a need, including the west coast. When Pigeon Point, CA needed a first order lens, the Lighthouse Board had one on hand, the light from the old Cape Hatteras tower, the light that the Union used as a replacement for the missing lens. Of course, no one really knew what lens this was at the time. When it was installed and turned on, the light began to blink its pattern, flashing its bright light, then waiting ten seconds, then blinking back on again. It was the same as the Cape Hatteras pattern. Rumors abounded about the source for the Pigeon Point light, and confusion set in. Essentially over time, no one was able to keep track of the path the missing lens had taken, even though it was right where it should be, shining over Cape Hatteras in a new brick tower, complete with its distinctive daymark, the black and white candy stripe that made it the most recognizable lighthouse in the country.

So the light blinked its way into the twentieth century. Originally placed a quarter of a mile away from the shoreline, by the 1930s waves were breaking at its base, and the lighthouse was in jeopardy of being eroded to the point of falling. The light was still important to mariners, so a new lighthouse was built on Hatteras Island. But this had none of the style of the tall brick tower. A skeleton frame of metal was built in 1937 on the sound side in Buxton Woods, along with a new light that sent out the same light pattern as the old, now unused, Fresnel light sitting atop the brick lighthouse tower. The brick tower became part of the National Park Service, but was not restored due to issues with the war effort during the 1940s.

During that time, the brick lighthouse was opened to visitors. While there was little to no tourism during and right after the Second World War, locals would often be able to go up to enjoy the view of the ocean and coast, as well as see the fancy Fresnel lens. Since there was no lighthouse keeper, and no funds to maintain the light, the lens fell into disrepair. People would be able to take pieces of the lens for souvenirs, or just for fun. Over time, the lens was dismantled piece by piece.

In 1950, with the beach grown back to a protective distance from the lighthouse, the brick tower was again put into use, but the Fresnel lens was both useless from vandalism and obsolete with the use of the brighter aerobeacon technology. It was removed from the tower the year before. The lens was unceremoniously stored at the Wright Brothers monument, and later at the abandoned Little Kinnakeet Lifesaving Station. All that time, no one realized that the lens that had been atop the new 1870 Cape Hatteras Lighthouse was the original first order Fresnel lens that had been installed in the old, original tower built in 1803.

It took a modern investigator to hunt down and find the true history of the lens. In 2002, Kevin Duffus, a North Carolina researcher, after following the legends and tales of the light's travels, finally figured out the truth of the matter. Searching North Carolina Archives, as well as documents from the National Archives and the Library of Congress, Duffus finally determined the whereabouts of what had become known as the Lost Light, the biggest lighthouse mystery in the United States. The lens was unearthed from storage, and finally found a home in the Graveyard of the Atlantic Museum.

Today, the light graces the lobby at the museum. It was restored with loving care by professional lampists and metalworkers in 2005, but without any replacement lenses to fill in the empty spots where the lens was vandalized. The intention is to use the display both to show the beauty of the Fresnel lens, as well as show how the selfish and callous acts of people can permanently damage the beauty of a wondrous machine that ultimately became a work of art.

Oddity

It is somewhat sad to see this lens, an object of great power, after it has been so ingloriously vandalized, but it still retains its mechanical beauty.

Difficulty ★

The lens and base are incredibly big, towering in the main lobby of the museum, just inside the doors.

Fresnel lenses greatly aided navigation for ships, as they amplified lights to a much greater degree than other lights in use at the time. A Fresnel lens would use over 80% of its light in projecting a beam, while the reflectors used before would only use 20-40% of its light source. A first order Fresnel lens could reach over 20 miles, almost to the horizon.

Ocracoke and Beyond

Ocracoke Ponies

Ocracoke 35.14855° -75.87158°

Going south from Nags Head through Cape Hatteras National Seashore, the touch of mankind slowly dwindles. Move from the developed beaches full of houses and people, into a coast connected only by a thin ribbon of asphalt, Highway 12, until you pass through some of the old villages on Hatteras Island, some built up, some still with the signs of times long past. But once the ferry leaves the docks at the end of Hatteras, it truly becomes a different world.

Ocracoke actually is in a different county than much of the Outer Banks. Crossing from the ferry at Hatteras, visitors enter into Hyde County. Much of Ocracoke is protected as part of the Cape Hatteras National Seashore, and it shows in that there is nothing but beach, dunes and natural plant growth across the entire island except for the village of Ocracoke. The tiny village still has most of its old charm, with few new buildings to be found there. Ocracoke is a step back in time.

And a long time ago, Ocracoke had some interesting visitors, who liked the place so much they stayed and made it home. Or maybe they did not have any choice. Either way, Ocracoke gained a herd of what would become known as Banker ponies.

No one is sure how the first ponies got to Ocracoke, but it could have happened as early as 1585, when Sir Richard Grenville, sailing toward Roanoke Island, may have put some stallions ashore in order to lighten the load on his ship *Tiger*, when it became grounded on a sandbar. It was common practice to throw animals and livestock overboard to lighten the load of a grounded ship, both due to the large weight of the animals, and probably because they could move on their own instead of having to push a crate over. The horses would swim or wade to shore, and, finding rather tasty vegetation upon which to feed, as well as a nice beach, they flourished on the island that would become Ocracoke.

Over the years, the horses became part of the landscape, along with settlers, fishermen, pirates, whoever found themselves on the island. The horses were used for riding, as well as for work, pulling boats and wagons. Soon, the locals began to claim the horses as their own. The small population made it easy for everyone to know whose horse was whose. The horses were never penned or tied. When the owner needed their horse, they just walked out to find it, and then let it go back into the wild when they were done. The horses needed no special care, no feed, no corrals, and thus, no expenses for the people on Ocracoke. Occasionally, a pony may stroll in through town or eat some plants in a garden, but mostly it was a mutually beneficial arrangement. The U.S. Coast guard even used Banker ponies to patrol beaches during World War II.

The ponies are visibly different than other horses. Ponies in name only, they really are full grown horses, but with distinct differences. They have a different number of ribs and vertebrae than other horses. They also have a different temperament, being a more docile animal. Due to this, the locals began claiming the horses with an annual pony penning, where they would be rounded up into the village and be branded or sold to people on the mainland who liked the Banker pony's even temperament. The horses were so prevalent, and so desirable, that even the local Boy Scout troop got involved with the ponies.

In the 1950s, the boys of Ocracoke were in need of an organized Boy Scout troop, as well as a leader for the troop. The task fell happily to Major Marvin Howard. Marvin, recently retired from a life of service for the Army Corps of Engineers, the US Navy, and the Army, was a native of Ocracoke, born in 1897 into the gale force winds of a tropical storm as it battered the island. Marvin would spend a good part of his life away from Ocracoke, but it was never far from his heart. After retirement, Marvin and his wife Leevella moved back to their home on the isolated barrier island. At this time, the pony penning had been going on in earnest, and Marvin was a large part of that event. But he wanted to bring his love of horses to more of the people of the island. When it was decided to have a Boy Scout troop, he not only took up the mantle of leadership, he also decided the troop would be mounted.

Troop 290 was formed from 14 teenagers who signed up in May of 1954. As part of membership in the group, each Scout had to raise $50 to purchase a horse for them to tame, ride, and care. While $50 was no small fee for a boy on the island, there were many jobs available for hard working young men at the time, and the Scouts were able to get their horses. At the time, this was the first and only mounted Boy Scout troop in existence. It took two scouts working together to break the wild ponies, one holding the horse, usually with a shirt over its eyes as a blindfold, while another scout would carefully place a saddle and bridle on the pony. The Scouts used their horses for trips across the roadless island, and even took them on the small ferry over to Hatteras Island for jamborees and campouts.

Regrettably, the joy of riding freely over the beach and dunes of Ocracoke Island would be short lived. The 1950s would be a time of change for the island. By 1957, a two lane road was built from the ferry docks at the north end of the island to the village on the south end of Ocracoke. On April 24, 1958, the Cape Hatteras National Seashore Park was dedicated. All of Ocracoke Island with the exception of the village was considered part of the National Park Service property. With the Park Service taking over the care of the island, it was intended to round up all the ponies from the island and remove them. The concern was that the horses would continue to thrive at the detriment of the native plants. Most other wild and feral non native animals, livestock, pigs, other grazing animals had already been removed. The government feared wild ponies running the beaches and the roads, causing accidents and injuries. Locals, including Marvin Howard and the local Scouts, petitioned to save the ponies by penning them. A compromise was reached, and money was raised for a pen and feed for the horses. For the first time in centuries, Banker ponies did not roam free on Ocracoke Island.

While penned in, the horses were cared for by the local Scouts. But ultimately the Scouts were required to carry insurance on their horses. The cost became insurmountable, and the Scouts that once were kids grew into adults with jobs and other concerns, often off the island. Care of the horses in the pen fell to the Park Service in the 1960s. By 1976, the herd was on the verge of extinction, with less than 10 animals left in the pen. During this time, the herd was managed to begin the resurrection of the herd, bringing back the ponies to a viable population.

Today, the horses are maintained at a populace of about 25 to 30 ponies, with breeding managed to create the best gene pool. The pen is located in the middle of the island, with a viewing platform available to see the once wild, once tame, horses that were as much the owners of Ocracoke Island as anyone.

Oddity ★

The pen is not fancy, but the horses are always visible playing and running in the large pen. The story of their history is pretty impressive to be contained in such a small piece of land.

Difficulty ★

The road to Ocracoke is a narrow one. The pen entrance is marked with a sign before the turnoff, as well as a beach access on the east side of the road. Always be careful on these narrow roads as people may be slamming on their brakes to make a turn, or just stopping in the street.

Live Oaks

Ocracoke

Howard Oak 35.11296° -75.98125°
Springer's Point 35.10586° -75.98641°

Throughout Ocracoke, one may see live oaks, which are twisted, large oak trees that grow well on the sound side of the Outer Banks. The trees have low extended branches that seem like they would be perfect for hanging pirates and brigands. The trees create that great blood chilling feeling that little kids get when thinking about bloodthirsty pirates of the past meeting their end in gruesome ways.

During colonial times, English representatives would buy the oaks for exorbitant prices that even reluctant landowners could not refuse. Then, when they had enough of the trees, they would tie the oaks together, and rather than ship them on sailing vessels, throw them into the ocean where the Gulf Stream would carry the trees all the way across the Atlantic to hopefully wash up on the shores of England to be used to build more ships.

While many of these majestic oaks ended up as the keels of British vessels, some have survived to be preserved and honored with their own society. The Live Oak Society was founded in 1934 by Dr. Edwin Stevens to promote the preservation and recognition of the tree. Ocracoke is home to several trees in the Society, including the enormous William Howard Oak, with coordinates given here. There are others along Howard Street as well. Two more member oaks are located in Springer's Point Land Trust, a preserve located to the south of the town. One of the oaks is the appropriately named Blackbeard's Oak, after the infamous pirate who met his end at Teach's Hole off of Springer's Point.

Oddity
Live oaks are hauntingly beautiful, with branches that tempt kids to climb, or, on a stormy night, may reach out to snatch passersby. Beware!

Difficulty ★★
Ocracoke is only accessible by ferry from Hatteras Island or Swan Quarter. Howard Street may be passable by car, but it is a narrow sand road, and better seen on foot. Springer's Point is accessible only by foot or bike, and has no parking at its entrance, or anywhere nearby, for that matter.

The reason why the name Howard is so prevalent on Ocracoke is because many of the residents descended from William Howard, owner of much of the island back in 1759. Howard's personal history is somewhat darker than his descendants. He was quartermaster for Blackbeard from 1717 to 1718.

British Cemetery

Ocracoke 35.11668° -75.98076°

The British Cemetery in Ocracoke is a well known attraction for visitors to Ocracoke village. It is easy to find, with signs marking the way, and the street is named British Cemetery Road. But there is always a little more to every story, especially this one.

At the beginning of World War II, the US was ill prepared to protect merchant ships from Nazi U-boats in the Atlantic. Most of the U.S. fleet was being used in the Pacific to chase down and defeat the Japanese navy. At the beginning of the war, only one Navy ship was tasked with defending the Atlantic coast.

With much needed supplies going to the bottom of the sea instead of to provision strapped Great Britain, the British came to the aid of its allies with a flotilla of converted fishing trawlers, used to detect submarines, sweep for mines, attack enemy subs with deck guns and depth charges, and guide other ships to their targets, keeping the German submarines away from merchant vessels.

One of those ships was the trawler HMT *Bedfordshire*. Retasked and renamed the HMS *Bedfordshire*, the ship was armed with a 4-inch deck gun, machine gun, and depth charges. Its job was to escort and protect ships sailing Diamond Shoals by Hatteras. On May 11, 1942, the German sub U-588 torpedoed and sank the *Bedfordshire*, which went down with all hands lost. On May 14, two bodies from the *Bedfordshire* washed ashore. The bodies were identified as *Bedfordshire* sailors by Aycock Brown, whose position with the US Navy was identifying bodies found at sea and preparing them for burial. In a strange twist, Brown was able to identify the sailors as from the *Bedfordshire* because he had talked with them only the week before. Brown had gone onboard the *Bedfordshire* in Morehead City and met with one of the officers, Sub-Lt. Thomas Cunningham. Brown had asked Cunningham for four British flags to drape over the coffins of British sailors. Cunningham gave Brown the four flags, plus two extra.

A week later, one of the bodies that Brown identified from the *Bedfordshire* would be Cunningham. Little did Cunningham know at the time that one of the two extra flags he gave Aycock Brown would have been used on his own coffin a week later. The other body was Telegraphist Stanley R. Craig. Two other bodies later recovered were never identified. The four bodies were buried in a small plot of land near Ocracoke harbor.

Originally, Ocracoke locals cared for the graves. Over the years, different groups and people have made sure the cemetery was well tended. Chief Boatswain's Mate Peter N. Stone of the U.S. Coast Guard did a lot of the care personally during his time stationed in Ocracoke as well as after he retired. Chief Stone has become an expert on the history of the *Bedfordshire* and the story of her sinking. The cemetery land was deeded to Great Britain through the Commonwealth War Graves Commission and the land is now considered British soil. The Coast Guard station and the Graveyard of the Atlantic Museum now take care of the cemetery.

All hands onboard the HMS *Bedfordshire* were lost during the torpedo attack, but there was one surviving crew member from the *Bedfordshire*. Crew member Sam Nutt missed the ship's departure at Morehead City because he had been assigned shore patrol. He wasn't released from his shore assignment until after the *Bedfordshire* departed. He boarded another British ship in order to catch up with the *Bedfordshire* at a predesignated rendezvous point and board it around Hatteras, but because the *Bedfordshire* got torpedoed, Nutt never found his ship at the rendezvous point. Since the ship was not known to be lost for three days by anyone else, Nutt probably was the first person to realize that his ship had been sunk.

Oddity ★

This is a very small, and very hallowed, piece of Britain in a sleepy pirate town.

Difficulty ★

Go through the town and turn right on British Cemetery Road, just past the Anchorage Inn. It couldn't be any easier. You will have to catch a ferry to Ocracoke Island, and going earlier in the day will mean less waiting time at the ferry docks.

The HMS *Bedfordshire* was only in service for two months off of Diamond Shoals before being sunk. The *Bedfordshire* had been working off the coast of Wales and had even chased off a U-boat that was attempting to torpedo a ship that was making a repair to the Trans-Atlantic Cable.

Teach's Hole

Ocracoke 35.10550° -75.98855°

A walk out to see Teach's Hole today is a pleasant stroll through Springer's Point, a nature preserve on the southern side of Ocracoke Village. Hike over to the sound side and look out over the peaceful water, its glassy surface unruffled by wind or wave. The bay at most times is a scene of peace and serenity. It is a hard thing to imagine this spot to be a watery abattoir where one of the most famous and bloodthirsty pirates of all time finally met his demise.

Edward Teach created the persona of Blackbeard as a ferocious, murderous buccaneer, whose name was to be feared throughout the Atlantic Ocean and Caribbean. After Queen Anne's War, Teach moved from privateering to piracy, like so many others who found themselves out of a lucrative job at the end of the hostilities between the English and the French. In 1716, Teach joined forces with noted pirate Benjamin Hornigold, and the two used their safe haven of New Providence in the Bahamas as a base to attack and pillage other ships. Teach spent much of the next two years pillaging ships throughout the waters of the New World. After holding the entire city of Charleston hostage in May of 1718 in order to receive medicine for his sick crew, Blackbeard decided to seek a pardon for his piracy, as many of the buccaneers were now being hunted down and hanged, their bodies left to rot at the mouth of many a harbor. Teach decided to attempt to receive the pardon from colonial governor Charles Eden of North Carolina, feeling he could trust the governor. But to be sure, he suggested to fellow pirate Stede Bonnet that Bonnet go first. While Bonnet was ashore at Bath getting his pardon, Teach was busy running two of his ships, including the *Queen Anne's Revenge*, aground, moving all the plunder to one sloop, effectively denying Bonnet of his share of the booty. Blackbeard then gained his own pardon from Eden in June of 1718, having a small fortune to keep him comfortable in the nominal capital of Bath.

But a life on land quickly becomes a grind, even for the newly married for the fourteenth time and quite wealthy Blackbeard. He was allowed passage to Ocracoke, where his sloop was kept, and also traveled to St. Thomas, allegedly to get a privateer's license, but more likely to return to piracy. By August, he had gained new ships for his flotilla. The governors of other coastal states began to worry that Blackbeard would return to his piratical ways, using Ocracoke as a lawless base to spy ships passing going north to Virginia and beyond. This concerned Virginia governor Alexander Spotswood. Governor Spotswood ordered Captain Brand of the HMS *Lyme* and Captain Gordon of the HMS *Pearl* to travel overland to Bath in order to capture the brigand. In order to cut off any escape by water, two sloops from the *Pearl* were to be commanded by a lieutenant from the *Pearl*, Robert Maynard. Maynard's name would go down in history, and Blackbeard's in infamy, for what would transpire next.

Blackbeard was not in Bath. His sloop, *Adventure*, was at rest on the soundside of sleepy Ocracoke. Maynard had searched out for Blackbeard, stopping ships to discover his whereabouts from other sailors. He located the pirate on the evening of November 21, 1718, aboard the *Adventure*. Unsure of the depth of the constantly shifting sandbars along Ocracoke's inlet, Maynard waited until daybreak to cross over toward Blackbeard in order to attack with his two ships, the *Jane* and the *Ranger*.

Early morning had Maynard approaching the notorious pirate. Blackbeard had been drinking the night before, but he apparently was up before the break of dawn. The two ships of Maynard's were easily spotted, and Blackbeard raised his skeleton crew. Most had been left in Bath, but the 25 men under Blackbeard's command rallied to the threat. Blackbeard cut the anchor to the *Adventure*, and made to close the gap between the ships, and get his guns within range. Blackbeard turned his ship so his starboard guns could rake the *Jane* and *Ranger*, and fired a devastating broadside. The effect was ruinous for Maynard. One of the ships was so shattered that it was unable to play any role in the fight. The blast sliced through wood, as well as flesh and bone, killing or wounding about 20 sailors aboard the *Jane*.

Maynard, having no big guns on his ship, resorted to small arms fire from muskets and pistols. The *Jane*, bludgeoned so severely by Blackbeard's broadside, retreated from the attack, leaving the *Ranger* alone to continue the attack. The *Adventure* may have had its jib damaged by a musket ball, and ran aground. The *Ranger*, with its crew unsure of the local waters, ran ashore on a sandbar. The race to free the ships was on, as each tried to lighten their load to float their ships. Blackbeard was able to finally release the *Adventure* from the sound floor and make his approach to the *Ranger* and Maynard. Blackbeard made it clear no quarter would be given.

Maynard prepared his men by having them go below decks, making the ship appear empty except for a few sailors. Blackbeard closed on the *Ranger*, grappled it, and after throwing some grenades over the deck, boarded the ship, with blood and death on his mind. He and his men discharged their flintlocks at Maynard and his small crew; Maynard replied in kind, his pistol bursting forth its own form of slaughter. The weapons spent, both crews drew their swords to deal death in the close quarters of Maynard's little sloop. Blackbeard approached the remnant sailors of the Ranger, its deck already slick with blood. Just as Blackbeard closed in on Maynard at the stern, the rest of the Ranger's crew burst forth from the hold, taking the pirates by surprise.

The pirates attempted to rally, but the newly superior numbers of Maynard's men pushed the pirates back toward the bow. In the battle, Blackbeard had managed to use his heavy cutlass to break Maynard's sword, but could not stop the ever encroaching group of sailors against the pirates. Blackbeard was now surrounded and isolated. Maynard stepped back in order to fire a pistol at Blackbeard. Seeing the imminent danger, Blackbeard charged the lieutenant, and one of Maynard's sailors struck a heavy blow against Blackbeard, severely slashing his neck. Gravely wounded, the rest of the men pounced. Blackbeard was killed in a savage attack, receiving 5 shots and 20 cuts from swords.

Edward Teach, Blackbeard the dreaded pirate, was dead. His legendary reign of terror would last less than two years. Maynard removed Blackbeard's head from his body and hung it from the bowsprit of his ship, a gory prize for a dirty job.

The rest of the pirates quickly gave up after seeing their captain fall. They were captured, taken to Virginia, tried and hanged. Their bodies were left to rot as a warning to other pirates and brigands who thought to follow in Blackbeard's sails.

Blackbeard may have only been the scourge of the seas for a few years, but his story became legendary. The many wounds he received at his last battle made for the legend that, even after having his head cut off and his body dumped overboard, his body swam around the boat three times hoping to find his head, reattach it, and continue the fight. Israel Hands, Blackbeard's second in command, escaped the noose because he had not taken part in the fight, and technically was still under a governor's pardon. His name would later go down in history as one of the pirates in Robert Louis Stevenson's Treasure Island. Blackbeard's severed head even became a part of legend and mystery. Supposedly his skull was covered in silver and turned into a chalice. Legends have the cup being used in several different secret societies, but there is no evidence of it actually existing outside of tall tales.

Blackbeard himself may still be around in several forms. It seems a man as devilish as Blackbeard may have been too frightening for even the Devil to take in, and Blackbeard's ghost wanders many locations. There are still tales of "Teach's Light" pacing the shores of Ocracoke, or his ship appearing in the mist. He is also seen as a ghostly orb around Plum Point, also named Teach's Point, in his last home at Bath. There is even the unlikely tale that Blackbeard haunts a promontory in Hampton Roads, VA.

Today, Teach's Hole is much more peaceful than back in Blackbeard's time. Visitors can walk out to the beach on Springer's Point to see the water where the battle took place early that fateful November morning. There are even kayak tours to go out in the water where the battle took place. Blackbeard has become a favorite son of sorts for the village of Ocracoke, where today's pirates young and old can enjoy the swashbuckling romance of the Golden Age of Piracy.

Oddity ★★

The area in the sound is just different looking, with its shallows and sandbars. Going out there and imagining seeing Blackbeard and Maynard battling in the morning light will send a few cold shivers up your spine.

Difficulty★★★

Ocracoke is accessible by ferry from either Hatteras or the mainland, and that can be a long wait as well as a long ride. Seeing Teach's Hole either means walking out to Springer's Point, which does not have a parking lot, or taking a kayak tour. The Ocracoke lighthouse is near, but not very near, and does not offer much in the way of parking. Renting a bike or kayak might be the best option.

Edward Teach built up a great reputation as the bloodthirsty pirate Blackbeard in only two years. No one knows much about him before his pirate days. He was probably only 38 years old when he was killed.

Most know of Blackbeard's real name, Edward Teach. He was also known by the name Thach, Thatch, Thack, and Tack, to name a few. But even that may have been made up. Blackbeard was probably from a well to do family. He was literate and highly intelligent. He may have made up the name Teach in order to protect his family name.

Blackbeard's ship, the *Adventure*, went missing into history. No one knows what happened to it. The same can be said of Blackbeard's body. It is assumed that his headless corpse was buried in a mass grave somewhere on Ocracoke Island. Watch your step.

Fort Ocracoke

Ocracoke 35.09765° -76.07287°

The beginnings of the Civil War were hardly auspicious in their successes, for neither the Union nor the Confederates. The South may have been enthusiastic in their desire to leave the nation, but they were woefully unprepared for the defense of the southern coastline. And the Union was certainly surprised by relative triumphs of the Confederates at Bull Run, as well as the attacks made on shipping by privateers such as the CSS *Winslow*. The *Winslow* operated out of the Cape Hatteras area, and took several prizes during her time as a Confederate ship. The Union Navy decided to do something about the rebel threat on the Carolina coast.

The mainland of North Carolina would be endangered if Union ships were able to enter the sound, so several small forts were built along the islands, including Fort Hatteras and Fort Clark, near Hatteras Inlet, to protect the inlet as an access for several inland ports to the Atlantic Ocean. Built of mostly sand and wood, the forts were meagerly equipped with whatever artillery they could get at the time, artillery that would never be the match of the Union's long range naval guns.

In August of 1861, some 800 troops under General Benjamin Butler trudged ashore to the hot windy bug infested beaches of Cape Hatteras to attack the forts, manned by about 580 Confederate soldiers. The Union soldiers were barely able to walk after their inglorious arrival, and their powder was wet and unusable. They did not have the strength to swat away the mosquitoes that sucked their blood, much less mount an attack. Fortunately for them, the Union fleet offshore was able to shell the two forts with impunity. The Confederates' weak artillery may have been able to deny entrance to Hatteras Inlet, but it had no reach out into the ocean. The Union ships rained death upon the Confederates hiding in the forts. After Fort Clark was pummeled, the soldiers retreated into Fort Hatteras. A small contingent of Union soldiers was able to take the now abandoned fort. Unfortunately, the fort was more than empty of enemy soldiers; it was empty of food as well. The soldiers spent a night starving in the summer heat.

The next morning, the shelling began afresh, this time upon Fort

Hatteras. Knowing what was to happen, the Confederate soldiers surrendered the fort after hours of shelling. The destruction of the forts and the opening of the Pamlico Sound to the Union ships meant that the mainland of eastern North Carolina was now ripe for the picking. Towns like Washington, New Bern, and Elizabeth City would soon fall. The Confederate Mosquito Fleet had nothing to match the might of the Union Navy. This would be the first victory for the Union forces, one that could be touted in newspapers across the north, to counter the bad news coming from inland.

The next target in the Union navy's sights was the fort guarding the entrance to the Pamlico Sound at Ocracoke Island. Fort Ocracoke, on Beacon Island, was in a superior location for a fort to guard the inlet. It sat on the interior of the inlet, away from the ocean, as well as away from the reach of the navy's large ship guns. The fort was well built, using mostly sand and wood to construct a heavy, thick stronghold. It was armed with eight-inch Columbiads and several 32 pound cannon. More barrels were to be placed on the fort once the carriages were available to mount them. If well stocked with powder and supplies, Fort Ocracoke would be formidable, and difficult to destroy. The fort rested in the shallows, where no large Union ship could approach, and with their guns at the fort, the Confederates could easily rake any small ship with explosives and hot shot, burning and destroying any craft that got near.

The only thing that could bring the fort down was the fear that crept into the minds of the soldiers stationed at the fort. After hearing of what had happened to the forts at Cape Hatteras, the small force that remained at Fort Ocracoke abandoned their base, leaving only six men behind to spike all the cannon and destroy the supplies. Then, they too, reluctantly left the fort for the relative safety of New Bern.

Once the Union found out that Fort Ocracoke had been abandoned, a ship was dispatched to make sure the fort was deserted, and to occupy Ocracoke as well. If the Confederate soldiers could have known what the Union troops described when they found Fort Ocracoke, they may not have given up without a fight. The schooner *Pawnee* went to Ocracoke Inlet, with the small steamer *Fanny*, in order to see what had happened at the fort. The *Fanny* was the only ship with a small enough draft to get close to Beacon Island and its shallow, shifting sandbars. The *Fanny* towed a small launch filled with men. Even the *Fanny* got stranded upon a sandbar, but the launch made its way to the fort. They found it empty, its guns spiked and useless. However, they reported that the shelters of timber were stout, and that the fort probably could have withstood any pounding from the small guns that could reach it. The fort would be unapproachable by the large ships of the Union fleet, and would have probably, if completed and well armed, kept the inlet from Union ships. It would have at least caused considerable damage to any ship willing to risk entering the treacherous inlet.

Unwilling to risk letting the fort ever get back into rebel hands, the Union marines from the launch set a torch to the remaining structures, utterly destroying the fort.

The fort has always been known to have existed on Beacon Island. Only recently has any remnant of the place been discovered. Local watermen noticed the remains of the fort and it was rediscovered in 1998.

Oddity★★★

Underwater ruins are always cool, even when there is little left of them. Shifting sands and tides may hide or uncover more. Who knows what you might find?

Difficulty★★★★★

To get out there, you'll need a boat, a kayak, maybe a submarine. And a calm day. You know, you could just stay around Ocracoke and eat a nice lunch, and just *say* you went out there, couldn't you? If you must see the location, you could try to take the Cedar Island ferry, as it may pass by the island if the channel is deep enough.

Portsmouth Ghost Town

Portsmouth Island 35.06980° -76.06381°

Windswept beaches, rolling dunes, empty, open, natural, these are all words used to describe the coast of North Carolina in its earliest state. When the islands were home only to the few hardy occupants and the animals that could flourish on the salt covered lands. Before the paved roads, the first hotels, before bridges. Before tourism, before people decided to pay hard earned money to sit in the sand and do nothing.

This is the picture some hold in their heads of what the islands were like before people came and civilized the land. Now, almost the entire coast is visited by locals and guests alike. Even sleepy Ocracoke has all the usual amenities one would want, not just the power and water, but cell phone connections, internet, high end food, nice hotels. But if you want to experience the way it was on the Outer Banks, you have to visit Portsmouth Island.

Portsmouth Island is just south of Ocracoke, across from the Ocracoke Inlet. Its tiny namesake town, Portsmouth, is only a collection of a dozen or so empty houses, including a one room school house and tiny church. But the emptiness and quietude belies a history of great depth. For in its day, Portsmouth was a viable and important part of the Atlantic seaboard, a vital link of land and sea.

Founded in 1753 as a planned town, with the buildings' locations laid out even before people lived there, Portsmouth quickly grew as a major maritime port. It served as a lightering port, a place where the large oceangoing ships could unload cargo onto smaller, shallow draft boats capable of passing through the shifting inlet and traversing the Pamlico Sound. Within 100 years, the village had grown to a population of over 500 residents, and 1400 ships came through the inlet every year. Portsmouth Island had become a vital and important part of naval commerce on the east coast. The island took a few blows, literally and figuratively, over the ensuing decades. In 1846, hurricanes opened the Oregon Inlet and deepened the passage at Hatteras Inlet. That, along with shoaling that occurred through Ocracoke Inlet, made Portsmouth Island less viable as a port. Soon after, the Civil War brought bloodshed to the island, and left with fewer people willing to return to Portsmouth Island. The steady decline was exacerbated in 1937, with another terrible hurricane season helping to reduce the population. The number of islanders dropped to three by 1971. Henry Pigott was an elderly fisherman and clammer, who took care of the two remaining ladies on the island, Nora Dixon and Marion Gray Babb. When Pigott died, the ladies reluctantly had to move away, and the island was abandoned to the whims of nature.

But Portsmouth was not abandoned for long. In 1976, the National Park Service formed the Cape Lookout National Seashore, and Portsmouth Island is the northernmost part of the preserve. Since the island is meant to be a natural and wild land, it is easy to keep it in its pure state. The remnants of the town are kept in a sense of arrested decay. There are a few homes, a Methodist church, a visitor center, the old general store and post office, and the life saving station, that still stand. The buildings are opened seasonally for tours.

Access to the island is difficult. With no bridges, and no roads, the only means of access is by ferry. From Ocracoke to Portsmouth Village the boat is for passengers only. There are ferries available from the south that will transport people and vehicles, but since there are no roads, four wheel drive is necessary. To visit the village, the best choice by far is to take the passenger ferry from Ocracoke, which puts in on the sound side beach. The paths to the village are dirt, which means they could be mud after a good rain. And the stories of the mosquitoes of Portsmouth Island are legendary.

But when you get there, when you see the village, even empty, it feels alive. The ghosts walk the town, right behind the back of the few visitors that come over every day. Portsmouth still has a life to it, a vibrancy that can be seen and felt. It is like there is a heartbeat in the sand, pulsing through the feet of every person who visits. It may not always be noticeable, but it is there. Portsmouth is not waiting for its people to come back. They always are there in spirit.

Oddity ★★★
It is a wonderful feeling to cross over to a different time. The place is not strange, just different. Pleasantly haunted would be a good phrase.

Difficulty ★★★★★
The only way over to the village is by a private passenger ferry, essentially a pontoon boat. You will need everything! Water, food, good walking shoes, a hat, bug spray, more bug spray, sunscreen, bug spray... The only bathrooms are at the visitor's center, as well as compost toilets near the life saving station. You may want to bring toilet paper, too. Just in case.

Camping is allowed on the beach and cabin rentals are available on the southern side with access by ferries from the towns of Atlantic and Davis. You really have to pack everything in and out if you do primitive camping. If you can hack it, the reward of a natural beach and a truly quiet night is worth the work.

The residents of Portsmouth Island actually built an artificial island in the inlet out of shells, similar to the oyster shell landbridge near Whalebone Junction. Known as Shell Castle, it was located near Fort Ocracoke and Beacon Island. There is nothing left of the island today.

Portsmouth Village has an event called Homecoming, originally meant for the resettled families from the local churches to come back to the island for a day. It has turned into a larger event run by the Park Service, which includes visitors not tied to the original inhabitants of the island. It happens once every two years, usually in April.

More Did You See That Detours

There are plenty of little diversions all along the coast. This book contains only a scoop of the many places to stop, either for an afternoon, or just for a minute. Here are a few other places to check out, with the coordinates and a bit of a description provided. Add them into a fun little scavenger hunt for the evening out.

Glenn Eure's Ghost Fleet Gallery is a treat, not just for the works that hang on the wall, but for Glenn himself. When he first built the gallery, he carved an anchor into the parking lot. See it at 35.98978° -75.64439°.

The house that is across the street from the Ghost Fleet Gallery, with the lighthouse on top? That originally belonged to Bruce Roberts. Bruce wrote books on lighthouses, and was the photographer for his former wife, Nancy Roberts, who wrote great books of the haunted tales of North Carolina and beyond.

The Roanoke Island Aquarium is a nice place to take the kids, or anybody, on a hot day. The cool dark rooms are a peaceful respite if you have a sunburn. But they also have a giant shark,, a giant shark tooth, and giant whale bones. 35.91819° - 75.70384°

Most totem poles are carved from a tall straight tree. But at the beach, they would of course be made of sand. See the Outer Banks Totem at 36.01166° - 75.661783°. It was made by Gary Colson, a Virginia sculptor and teacher. The totem sits in front of the Baum Center, and is part of the nice walking path that is the Outer Banks Arboretum. Take a walk through to see some other neat art, and don't just look around, look down. Some of the walkway is painted or imprinted with leaves and plants.

If you are looking for a good coastal scavenger hunt, see how many nautical items you can find while out going from place to place. There are at least a few large anchors, numerous buoys, some stranded boats, a shipwreck or two, and even a screw pile from a lighthouse somewhere along the islands of the Outer Banks. By the way, the big round buoys are called mooring buoys. They would be placed in a harbor with an anchor, and meant for boats to moor up to them instead of come to a dock. Buoys with lights on them usually marked channels. You can even see a giant propeller at Pirate's Quay shopping center at 35.97587° -75.64038°.

Shipwrecks were a common occurrence on the coast, but unless you

have a boat and a scuba tank, you may not see any unless you know where to look. Spot one right on the beach in Kill Devil Hills at 36.02658° -75.66258°. If you go out to Pea Island, and walk out onto the beach, a small part of the ship *Oriental*, also known as the Boiler Wreck is visible offshore at 35.71877° -75.48889°. Farther south, in Salvo, just offshore is the *Pocahontas*, an old side wheel paddle steamer lost during the Civil War. See its giant axle and engine at 35.54113° -75.46439°

What are those windmills doing on the Outer Banks? Most are making electric power, at Outer Banks Brew Pub and Jennette's Pier. But one is a bit different. Now in Manteo at the Roanoke Island Farm, this windmill used to sit at Lynanne Wescott's shop on the Nags Head sound. Once a gift shop that sold ground flour and meal, it later was turned into a restaurant known as Windmill Point, and had many of the fancy interior decorations from the SS *United States* cruise ship, including the ship's bar. The property was sold and is now used as an event park for Nags Head, and the windmill was moved to Manteo. But why a windmill? Well, there was, and still is, a lot of free wind power on the Outer Banks. Instead of grinding grains inland and then shipping the flour out on ships, the grains were brought to the beach, ground in the many windmills there, and then shipped as flour. See the windmill at 35.92938° - 75.68682°. The Island Farm is also a nice place to visit, across the street. There is an admission fee to see the farm.

Built in 1898, the old Lifesaving Station on the south end of Oregon Inlet sat in disrepair after being vacated in 1988. It was a decaying landmark until being restored on the outside.and raised up on pilings. Now it is a popular spot for sunset photos. It is easily accessed by a short hike from the parking lot at the south end of the new Marc Basnight Bridge over Oregon Inlet. Find it at 35.7679° -75.52375°

Afterword

"We could have spent every day of the summer just sitting on the beach."

It's only been about six years since I wrote this book, but somehow it seems so long ago. That's about two thousand sunsets into the sound behind Jockey's Ridge. Times change, and so does the coast. For good or bad, the Outer Banks evolves. What we lost helped us see the value of what we have. I looked at the things that aren't there anymore, the several Flat Top houses in Southern Shores, plus the other houses, unnoticed, in other towns, that were torn down, the little bit of art on the road in Kitty Hawk, the big shark at Jennette's Pier, all gone. But there are four houses now preserved on the Register of Historic Places. We have a smooth new road down the beach. There's another fish up to see.

That's the way it is on an island that is moving and changing. It doesn't sit still even if we try to hold down the sand by just sitting on the beach every day.

We survived the storms, floods, and hurricanes that are part of the coast. We dealt with the unpredictability of time and tide. Some things just change. Some things don't, however.

The kiteboarders still show up down near Hatteras. Oregon Inlet still sparkles and churns in the late afternoon light. Shells still litter the beaches. The lights still come on at twilight at our lighthouses. The sun will sink into the water under an orange sky.

We even got a few nice additions. Oregon Inlet got a new bridge. And a restored piece of history in its lifesaving station. New parks and hiking paths were built. The Outer Banks no longer lives from June to the first hurricane in September like it did when I was a kid.

In my original afterword I encouraged people not to just sit on the beach, but to get out and find the places in this book. Now I think we need no encouragement. We want to get out and see what's out there. We want an adventure. There is value in that discovery, that time spent together to find something new and different. When you go to the places in this book, be on the lookout for the other places. Look for the signs, the shops, the chances to take, the things you can only do here. Whether you live on the beach or vacation here, make the Outer Banks an adventure.

Joe Sledge Jan 2021

Further Reading

Vintage Outer Banks: Shifting Sands & Bygone Beaches by Sarah Downing

Hidden History of the Outer Banks by Sarah Downing

How to Read a North Carolina Beach: Bubbled Holes, Barking Sands, and Rippled Runnels by Orrin H. Pilkey, Tracy Monegan Rice, and William J. Neal.
Legends of the Outer Banks and Tarheel Tidewater by Charles H. Whedbee

The Lost Light by Kevin Duffus

Landmarks of the Northern Outer Banks by Jack Dudley

The Unpainted Aristocracy: The Beach Cottages of Old Nags Head by Catherine
W. Bishir

The Outer Banks of North Carolina, 1954-1958 by David Stick

The Ash Wednesday Storm by David Stick

Aycock Brown's Outer Banks by David Stick

For further research and information, check out these web sites

Want to tour the Whalehead Club? Look for events
there at http://www.visitwhalehead.com/.
See several of the Flat Top cottages of Southern Shores at
https://www.facebook.com/pages/Southern-Shores-Historic-
Flat-Top- Cottages/421136131314749/ .
Want to check out the surf? See if it is storming? Locals and visitors alike go
to Avalon Fishing Pier's webcam at http://www.avalonpier.com/piercam.html.
For detailed information on events, as well as the daily fishing report and
water temps, see http://www.jennettespier.net/.
The Outer Banks History Center, at Festival Park, has both online and
onsite research available to hardcore searchers of history, both
ancient and recent. See their online database at
http://www.ncdcr.gov/archives/Public/OuterBanksHistoryCenter.aspx.
The Elizabethan Gardens are always open, but you can see what is in
bloom on their website at http://elizabethangardens.org/.
Events at Alligator River NWR and Pea Island can be
found at http://www.fws.gov/alligatorriver/spec.html.
There are lots of great pieces of maritime history to be seen at the
Graveyard of the Atlantic Museum down in Hatteras, as well as on their
site at http://www.graveyardoftheatlantic.com/index.htm.
For information on ferries to the Cape Lookout Seashore, including
Portsmouth Island, see http://www.nps.gov/calo/planyourvisit/ferry.htm.
To get an idea of the changes over the centuries that the Outer Banks
has been through, including older inlets and original place names, try
searching for "Outer Banks" on the North Carolina maps page, at
http://www2.lib.unc.edu/dc/ncmaps/ .

Acknowledgements

In writing this, or any work of nonfiction, there are always a number of people to thank. Without their help and information, this book would have been much less than what it is.

Scooter Lewis for his help in the history of the SOSUS cables in Hatteras, as well as all the other good stories, Danny Couch at Hatteras Tours and Susan Grey at the Fessenden Center for pointing me in the right direction for the Fessenden remains, Clara Scarborough at the Graveyard of the Atlantic Museum for helping to explain the convoluted history of the Cape Hatteras Lighthouses, Jay Bender for giving some history on Penny's Hill, Denise Wells from the Outer Banks Community Foundation for her information on the Flat Top houses of Southern Shores, Jill Landen from the Whalehead Club, Lee McMaster at the Elizabethan Gardens, Stuart Parks and Sarah Downing at the Outer Banks History Center for all the searches for pictures of that NASA dish, Barry Wickre at Creef Boatworks for information on the shad boat tours. Thanks to all of you for all the help you gave in fleshing this book out.

Photo Credits

All photos by Joe Sledge except where noted below. All photos used with permission or granted through public domain or creative commons license. Permission is granted for use in this book only, and does not constitute any endorsement of the work.

Penny's Hill – John B. Sledge, Jr.

Monkey Island courtesy of Blair Whitfield

Corolla Lighthouse (B&W) - Public Domain from U.S. Coast Guard archives Wright Brothers Monument in Kitty Hawk - Joyce Sledge Kellogg's Big Chair - Joyce Sledge

Red Wolf courtesy of U.S. Fish and Wildlife Service, released into Creative Commons (see license at https://creativecommons.org/licenses/by/2.0/) Whalebone Junction – public domain

NASA Tracking Dish – Aycock Brown, courtesy of the Outer Banks History Center
Nights in Rodanthe House – Michelle
Sledge Ocracoke Ponies –Joyce Sledge
Live Oaks –John Sledge III

British Cemetery at Ocracoke – Joyce Sledge

Teach's Hole – Casey Robinson, released into Creative Commons (see license at https://creativecommons.org/licenses/by/2.0/)
Fort Ocracoke courtesy John Buie

Portsmouth Island – National Park Service archives

About The Author

Joe Sledge is a North Carolina native and graduate of the University of North Carolina at Chapel Hill, where he developed a love for exploring. A native of the Outer Banks, Joe traveled across the country and lived in Monterey, CA, where he married his wife, Michelle. After ten years on the west coast, they moved back to North Carolina and currently live in the Piedmont, with their daughter. Joe worked for nine years as a special education teacher before writing this book. He and his family find any excuse to go to the beach or travel throughout the state. This is his second book in the ever growing Did You See That? series. Joe Has also edited and annotated a new version of *Nag's Head: Or, Two Months Among The Breakers*, by Gregory Seaworthy. Written in 1859, it was the first book that described the vacation life of the Outer Banks. He also has written fiction, the first in a series for young readers, written for his daughter, the book *Bess Truly And Her Zap-Gun Rangers*.

Made in the USA
Columbia, SC
23 May 2022

60828709R00109